Minnesota Twins 2020

A Baseball Companion

Edited by R.J. Anderson, Craig Goldstein and Bret Sayre

Baseball Prospectus

Craig Brown, Steven Goldman and David Pease, Consultant Editors
Robert Au, Harry Pavlidis and Amy Pircher, Statistics Editors

Copyright © 2020 by DIY Baseball, LLC.
All rights reserved

This book or any part thereof may not be reproduced or transmitted in any form or by any means, electronic or mechanical, including photocopying, recording, or by any information storage and retrieval system, without permission in writing from the publisher.

Limit of Liability/Disclaimer of Warranty: While the publisher and the author have used their best efforts in preparing this book, they make no representations or warranties with respect to the accuracy or completeness of the contents of this book and specifically disclaim any implied warranties of merchantability or fitness for a particular purpose. No warranty may be created or extended by sales representatives or written sales materials. The advice and strategies contained herein may not be suitable for your situation. You should consult with a professional where appropriate. Neither the publisher nor the author shall be liable for any loss of profit or any other commercial damages, including but not limited to special, incidental, consequential, or other damages.

Library of Congress Cataloging-in-Publication Data:
paperback
ISBN-13: 978-1-949332-80-3

Project Credits
Cover Design: Michael Byzewski at Aesthetic Apparatus
Interior Design and Production: Jeff Pease, Dave Pease
Layout: Jeff Pease, Dave Pease

Baseball icon courtesy of Uberux, from https://www.shareicon.net/author/uberux

Ballpark diagram courtesy of Lou Spirito/THIRTY81 Project, https://thirty81project.com/

Manufactured in the United States of America
10 9 8 7 6 5 4 3 2 1

Table of Contents

Statistical Introduction v

Part 1: Team Analysis

Minnesota Twins: Where Are You Going, Where Have You Been? 3
David Lesky, Keanan Lamb and Matthew Trueblood

Performance Graphs 7

2019 Team Performance 8

2020 Team Projections 9

Team Personnel 10

Target Field Stats 11

Twins Team Analysis 13

Part 2: Player Analysis

Twins Player Analysis 18

Twins Prospects 109

Part 3: Featured Articles

The Baseball Is Juiced (Again) 125
Robert Arthur

The Moral Hazard of Playing It Safe 129
Craig Goldstein

Index of Names 135

Statistical Introduction

Sports are, fundamentally, a blend of athletic endeavor and storytelling. Baseball, like any other sport, tells its stories in so many ways: in the arc of a game from the stands or a season from the box scores, in photos, or even in numbers. At Baseball Prospectus, we understand that statistics don't replace observation or any of baseball's stories, but complement everything else that makes the game so much fun.

What stats help us with is with patterns and precision, variance and value. This book can help you learn things you may not see from watching a game or hundred, whether it's the path of a career over time or the breadth of the entire MLB. We'd also never ask you to choose between our numbers and the experience of viewing a game from the cheap seats or the comfort of your home; our publication combines running the numbers with observations and wisdom from some of the brightest minds we can find. But if you *do* want to learn more about the numbers beyond what's on the backs of player jerseys, let us help explain.

Offense

We've revised our methodology for determining batting value. Long-time readers of the book will notice that we've retired True Average in favor of a new metric: Deserved Runs Created Plus (DRC+). Developed by Jonathan Judge and our stats team, this statistic measures everything a player does at the plate–reaching base, hitting for power, making outs, and moving runners over–and puts it on a scale where 100 equals league-average performance. A DRC+ of 150 is terrific, a DRC+ of 100 is average and a DRC+ of 75 means you better be an excellent defender.

DRC+ also does a better job than any of our previous metrics in taking contextual factors into account. The model adjusts for how the park affects performance, but also for things like the talent of the opposing pitcher, value of different types of batted-ball events, league, temperature and other factors. It's able to describe a player's expected offensive contribution than any other statistic we've found over the years, and also does a better job of predicting future performance as well.

There's a lot more to DRC+'s story, and you can read all about it in greater depth near the end of this book.

The other aspect of run-scoring is baserunning, which we quantify using Baserunning Runs. BRR not only records the value of stolen bases (or getting caught in the act), but also accounts for all the stuff that doesn't show up on the back of a baseball card: a runner's ability to go first to third on a single, or advance on a fly ball.

Defense

Where offensive value is *relatively* easy to identify and understand, defensive value is…not. Over the past dozen years, the sabermetric community has focused mostly on stats based on zone data: a real-live human person records the type of batted ball and estimated landing location, and models are created that give expected outs. From there, you can compare fielders' actual outs to those expected ones. Simple, right?

Unfortunately, zone data has two major issues. First, zone data is recorded by commercial data providers who keep the raw data private unless you pay for it. (All the statistics we build in this book and on our website use public data as inputs.) That hurts our ability to test assumptions or duplicate results. Second, over the years it has become apparent that there's quite a bit of "noise" in zone-based fielding analysis. Sometimes the conclusions drawn from zone data don't hold up to scrutiny, and sometimes the different data provided by different providers don't look anything alike, giving wildly different results. Sometimes the hard-working professional stringers or scorers might unknowingly inflict unconscious bias into the mix: for example good fielders will often be credited with more expected outs despite the data, and ballparks with high press boxes tend to score more line drives than ones with a lower press box.

Enter our Fielding Runs Above Average (FRAA). For most positions, FRAA is built from play-by-play data, which allows us to avoid the subjectivity found in many other fielding metrics. The idea is this: count how many fielding plays are made by a given player and compare that to expected plays for an average fielder at their position (based on pitcher ground ball tendencies and batter handedness). Then we adjust for park and base-out situations.

When it comes to catchers, our methodology is a little different thanks to the laundry list of responsibilities they're tasked with beyond just, well, catching and throwing the ball. By now you've probably heard about "framing" or the art of making umpires more likely to call balls outside the strike zone for strikes. To put this into one tidy number, we incorporate pitch tracking data (for the years it exists) and adjust for important factors like pitcher, umpire, batter and home-field advantage using a mixed-model approach. This grants us a number for how many strikes the catcher is personally adding to (or subtracting from) his pitchers' performance…which we then convert to runs added or lost using linear weights.

Framing is one of the biggest parts of determining catcher value, but we also take into account blocking balls from going past, whether a scorer deems it a passed ball or a wild pitch. We use a similar approach—one that really benefits from the pitch tracking data that tells us what ends up in the dirt and what doesn't. We also include a catcher's ability to prevent stolen bases and how well they field balls in play, and *finally* we come up with our FRAA for catchers.

Pitching

Both pitching and fielding make up the half of baseball that isn't run scoring: run prevention. Separating pitching from fielding is a tough task, and most recent pitching analysis has branched off from Voros McCracken's famous (and controversial) statement, "There is little if any difference among major-league pitchers in their ability to prevent hits on balls hit in the field of play." The research of the analytic community has validated this to some extent, and there are a host of "defense-independent" pitching measures that have been developed to try and extract the effect of the defense behind a hurler from the pitcher's work.

Our solution to this quandary is Deserved Run Average (DRA), our core pitching metric. DRA looks like earned run average (ERA), the tried-and-true pitching stat you've seen on every baseball broadcast or box score from the past century, but it's very different. To start, DRA takes an event-by-event look at what the pitchers does, and adjusts the value of that event based on different environmental factors like park, batter, catcher, umpire, base-out situation, run differential, inning, defense, home field advantage, pitcher role and temperature. That mixed model gives us a pitcher's expected contribution, similar to what we do for our DRC+ model for hitters and FRAA model for catchers. (Oh, and we also consider the pitcher's effect on basestealing and on balls getting past the catcher.)

It's important to note that DRA is set to the scale of runs allowed per nine innings (RA9) instead of ERA, which makes DRA's scale slightly higher than ERA's. The reason for this is because ERA tends to overrate three types of pitchers:

1. Pitchers who play in parks where scorers hand out more errors. Official scorers differ significantly in the frequency at which they assign errors to fielders.
2. Ground-ball pitchers, because a substantial proportion of errors occur on groundballs.
3. Pitchers who aren't very good. Better pitchers often allow fewer unearned runs than bad pitchers, because good pitchers tend to find ways to get out of jams.

Since the last time you picked up an edition of this book, we've also made a few minor changes to DRA to make it better. Recent research into "tunneling"—the act of throwing consecutive pitches that appear similar from a batter's point of view until after the swing decision point–data has given us a new contextual factor to account for in DRA: plate distance. This refers to the distance between successive pitches as they approach the plate, and while it has a smaller effect than factors like velocity or whiff rate, it still can help explain pitcher strikeout rate in our model.

New Pitching Metrics for 2020

We're including a few "new" pitching metrics in the book for the 2020 edition, though unlike last year, these numbers may be a little bit more familiar to those of you who have spent some time investigating baseball statistics.

Fastball Percentage

Our fastball percentage (FB%) statistic measures how frequently a pitcher throws a pitch classified as a "fastball," measured as a percentage of overall pitches thrown. We qualify three types of fastballs:

1. The traditional four-seam fastball;
2. The two-seam fastball or sinker;
3. "Hard cutters," which are pitches that have the movement profile of a cut fastball and are used as the pitcher's primary offering or in place of a more traditional fastball.

For example, a pitcher with a FB% of 67 throws any combination of these three pitches about two-thirds of the time.

Whiff Rate

Everybody loves a swing and a miss, and whiff rate (WHF) measures how frequently pitchers induce a swinging strike. To calculate WHF, we add up all the pitches thrown that ended with a swinging strike, then divide that number by a pitcher's total pitches thrown. Most often, high whiff rates correlate with high strikeout rates (and overall effective pitcher performance).

Called Strike Probability

Called Strike Probability (CSP) is a number that represents the likelihood that all of a pitcher's pitches will be called a strike while controlling for location, pitcher and batter handedness, umpire and count. Here's how it works: on each pitch, our model determines how many times (out of 100) that a similar pitch was called for a strike given those factors mentioned above, and when normalized for each batter's strike zone. Then we average the CSP for all pitches thrown by a pitcher in a season, and that gives us the yearly CSP percentage you see in the stats boxes.

As you might imagine, pitchers with a higher CSP are more likely to work in the zone, where pitchers with a lower CSP are likely locating their pitches outside the normal strike zone, for better or for worse.

Projections

Many of you aren't turning to this book just for a look at what a player has done, but for a look at what a player is going to do: the PECOTA projections. PECOTA, initially developed by Nate Silver (who has moved on to greater fame as a political analyst), consists of three parts:

1. Major-league equivalencies, which use minor-league statistics to project how a player will perform in the major leagues;
2. Baseline forecasts, which use weighted averages and regression to the mean to estimate a player's current true talent level; and
3. Aging curves, which uses the career paths of comparable players to estimate how a player's statistics are likely to change over time.

With all those important things covered, let's take a look at what's in the book this year.

Team Prospectus

Most of this book is composed of team chapters, with one for each of the 30 major-league franchises. On the first page of each chapter, you'll see a box that contains some of the key statistics for each team as well as a very inviting stadium diagram. (You can see an example of this for the Milwaukee Brewers on this very page!)

We start with the team name, their unadjusted 2019 win-loss record, and their divisional ranking. Beneath that are a host of other team statistics. **Pythag** presents an adjusted 2019 winning percentage, calculated by taking runs scored per game (**RS/G**) and runs allowed per game (**RA/G**) for the team, and running them through a version of Bill James' Pythagorean formula that was refined and improved by David Smyth and Brandon Heipp. (The formula is called "Pythagenpat," which is equally fun to type and to say.)

Next up is **DRC+**, described earlier, to indicate the overall hitting ability of the team either above or below league-average. Run prevention on the pitching side is covered by **DRA** (also mentioned earlier) and another metric: Fielding Independent Pitching (**FIP**), which calculates another ERA-like statistic based on strikeouts, walks, and home runs recorded. Defensive Efficiency Rating (**DER**) tells us the percentage of balls in play turned into outs for the team, and is a quick fielding shorthand that rounds out run prevention.

After that, we have several measures related to roster composition, as opposed to on-field performance. **B-Age** and **P-Age** tell us the average age of a team's batters and pitchers, respectively. **Salary** is the combined team payroll for all on-field players, and Doug Pappas' Marginal Dollars per Marginal Win (**M$/MW**) tells us how much money a team spent to earn production above replacement level.

Ending this batch of statistics is the number of disabled list days a team had over the season (**IL Days**) and the amount of salary paid to players on the disabled list (**$ on IL**); this final number is expressed as a percentage of total payroll.

Next to each of these stats, we've listed each team's MLB rank in that category from first to 30th. In this, first always indicates a positive outcome and 30th a negative outcome, except in the case of salary—first is highest.

After the franchise statistics, we share a few items about the team's home ballpark. There's the aforementioned diagram of the park's dimensions (including distances to the outfield wall), a graphic showing the height of the wall from the left-field pole to the right-field pole, and a table showing three-year park factors for the stadium. The park factors are displayed as indexes where 100 is average, 110 means that the park inflates the statistic in question by 10 percent, and 90 means that the park deflates the statistic in question by 10 percent.

On the second page of each team chapter, you'll find three graphs. The first is the **2019 Hit List Ranking**. This shows our Hit List Rank for the team on each day of the 2019 season and is intended to give you a picture of the ups and downs of the team's season. Hit List Rank measures overall team performance and drives the Hit List Power Rankings at the baseballprospectus.com website.

The second graph is **Committed Payroll** and helps you see how the team's payroll has compared to the MLB and divisional average payrolls over time. Payroll figures are current as of January 1, 2020; with so many free agents still unsigned as of this writing, the final 2020 figure will likely be significantly different for many teams. (In the meantime, you can always find the most current data at Baseball Prospectus' Cot's Baseball Contracts page.)

The third graph is **Farm System Ranking** and displays how the Baseball Prospectus prospect team has ranked the organization's farm system since 2007.

After the graphs, we have a **Personnel** section that lists many of the important decision-makers and upper-level field and operations staff members for the franchise, as well as any former Baseball Prospectus staff members who are currently part of the organization. (In very rare circumstances, someone might be on both lists!)

Juan Soto LF

Born: 10/25/98   Age: 21   Bats: L   Throws: L
Height: 6'1"   Weight: 185   Origin: International Free Agent, 2015

YEAR	TEAM	LVL	AGE	PA	R	2B	3B	HR	RBI	BB	K	SB	CS	AVG/OBP/SLG
2017	NAT	RK	18	27	3	1	1	0	4	2	1	0	0	.320/.370/.440
2017	HAG	A	18	96	15	5	0	3	14	10	8	1	2	.360/.427/.523
2018	HAG	A	19	74	12	5	3	5	24	14	13	2	0	.373/.486/.814
2018	POT	A+	19	73	17	3	1	7	18	11	8	0	1	.371/.466/.790
2018	HAR	AA	19	35	4	2	0	2	10	4	7	1	0	.323/.400/.581
2018	WAS	MLB	19	494	77	25	1	22	70	79	99	5	2	.292/.406/.517
2019	WAS	MLB	20	659	110	32	5	34	110	108	132	12	1	.282/.401/.548
2020	WAS	MLB	21	630	92	30	3	35	102	85	123	5	2	.284/.382/.543

Comparables: Ronald Acuña Jr., Mike Trout, Tony Conigliaro

YEAR	TEAM	LVL	AGE	PA	DRC+	VORP	BABIP	BRR	FRAA	WARP
2017	NAT	RK	18	27	135	1.5	.333	0.0	RF(9): -1.1	0.0
2017	HAG	A	18	96	181	8.0	.373	1.0	RF(19): -1.9, LF(2): -0.3	0.9
2018	HAG	A	19	74	222	14.5	.405	0.3	RF(14): 1.1, CF(2): 0.2	1.2
2018	POT	A+	19	73	260	15.4	.340	1.4	RF(14): 1.0, LF(1): 0.0	1.6
2018	HAR	AA	19	35	113	3.6	.364	0.0	LF(4): 0.6, RF(4): -0.5	0.1
2018	WAS	MLB	19	494	125	40.5	.338	-0.5	LF(114): 2.7	3.0
2019	WAS	MLB	20	659	136	49.0	.312	1.4	LF(150): -0.8	4.9
2020	WAS	MLB	21	630	133	43.6	.310	-0.1	LF 3	4.8

Position Players

After all that information and a thoughtful bylined essay covering each team, we present our player comments. These are also bylined, but due to frequent franchise shifts during the offseason, our bylines are more a rough guide than a perfect accounting of who wrote what.

Each player is listed with the major-league team that employed him as of early January 2020. If a player changed teams after that point via free agency, trade, or any other method, you'll be able to find them in the chapter for their previous squad.

As an example, take a look at the player comment for Nationals outfielder Juan Soto: the stat block that accompanies his written comment is at the top of this page. First we cover biographical information (age is as of June 30, 2020) before moving onto the stats themselves. Our statistic columns include standard identifying information like **YEAR**, **TEAM**, **LVL** (level of affiliated play) and **AGE** before getting into the numbers. Next, we provide raw, untranslated numbers like you might find on the back of your dad's baseball cards: **PA** (plate appearances), **R** (runs), **2B** (doubles), **3B** (triples), **HR** (home runs), **RBI** (runs batted in), **BB** (walks), **K** (strikeouts), **SB** (stolen bases) and **CS** (caught stealing).

Next, we have unadjusted "slash" statistics: **AVG** (batting average), **OBP** (on-base percentage) and **SLG** (slugging percentage). Following the slash line is **DRC+** (Deserved Runs Created Plus), which we described earlier as total offensive expected contribution compared to the league average.

One of our oldest active metrics, **VORP** (Value Over Replacement Player), considers offensive production, position and plate appearances. In essence, it is the number of runs contributed beyond what a replacement-level player at the same position would contribute if given the same percentage of team plate appearances. VORP does not consider the quality of a player's defense.

BABIP (batting average on balls in play) tells us how often a ball in play fell for a hit, and can help us identify whether a batter may have been lucky or not...but note that high BABIPs also tend to follow the great hitters of our time, as well as speedy singles hitters who put the ball on the ground.

The next item is **BRR** (Baserunning Runs), which covers all of a player's baserunning accomplishments including (but not limited to) swiped bags and failed attempts. Next is **FRAA** (Fielding Runs Above Average), which also includes the number of games previously played at each position noted in parentheses. Multi-position players have only their two most frequent positions listed here, but their total FRAA number reflects all positions played.

Our last column here is **WARP** (Wins Above Replacement Player). WARP estimates the total value of a player, which means for hitters it takes into account hitting runs above average (calculated using the DRC+ model), BRR and FRAA. Then, it makes an adjustment for positions played and gives the player a credit for plate appearances based upon the difference between "replacement level"—which is derived from the quality of players added to a team's roster after the start of the season–and the league average.

The final line just below the stats box is **PECOTA** data, which is discussed further in a following section.

Catchers

Catchers are a special breed, and thus they have earned their own separate box which displays some of the defensive metrics that we've built just for them. As an example, let's check out J.T. Realmuto.

The **YEAR** and **TEAM** columns match what you'd find in the other stat box. **P. COUNT** indicates the number of pitches thrown while the catcher was behind the plate, including swinging strikes, fouls and balls in play. **FRM RUNS** is the total run value the catcher provided (or cost) his team by influencing the umpire to call strikes where other catchers did not. **BLK RUNS** expresses the total run value above or below average for the catcher's ability to prevent wild pitches and passed balls. **THRW RUNS** is calculated using a similar model as the previous two statistics, and it measures a catcher's ability to throw out basestealers but also to dissuade them from testing his arm in the first place. It takes into account factors like the pitcher (including his delivery and pickoff move) and baserunner (who could be as fast as Billy Hamilton or as slow as Yonder Alonso). **TOT RUNS** is the sum of all of the previous three statistics.

Justin Verlander   RHP
Born: 02/20/83   Age: 37   Bats: R   Throws: R
Height: 6'5"   Weight: 225   Origin: Round 1, 2004 Draft (#2 overall)

YEAR	TEAM	LVL	AGE	W	L	SV	G	GS	IP	H	HR	BB/9	K/9	K	GB%	BABIP
2017	DET	MLB	34	10	8	0	28	28	172	153	23	3.5	9.2	176	34%	.283
2017	HOU	MLB	34	5	0	0	5	5	34	17	4	1.3	11.4	43	32%	.194
2018	HOU	MLB	35	16	9	0	34	34	214	156	28	1.6	12.2	290	31%	.272
2019	HOU	MLB	36	21	6	0	34	34	223	137	36	1.7	12.1	300	36%	.219
2020	HOU	MLB	37	15	6	0	29	29	184	138	28	2.3	12.1	248	35%	.274

Comparables: Zack Greinke, A.J. Burnett, Aníbal Sánchez

YEAR	TEAM	LVL	AGE	WHIP	ERA	DRA	WARP	MPH	FB%	WHF	CSP
2017	DET	MLB	34	1.28	3.82	4.03	3.0	97.7	58	11	47.8
2017	HOU	MLB	34	0.65	1.06	3.08	0.9	97.5	59.6	15.1	49.9
2018	HOU	MLB	35	0.90	2.52	2.33	7.3	97.5	61.2	16.2	51.6
2019	HOU	MLB	36	0.80	2.58	2.51	7.9	96.8	49.9	17.5	48.3
2020	HOU	MLB	37	1.01	2.75	2.95	5.3	95.8	54.6	15.1	48.2

Pitchers

Let's give our pitchers a turn, using 2019 AL Cy Young winner Justin Verlander as our example. Take a look at his stat block: the first line and the **YEAR**, **TEAM**, **LVL** and **AGE** columns are the same as in the position player example earlier.

Here too, we have a series of columns that display raw, unadjusted statistics compiled by the pitcher over the course of a season: **W** (wins), **L** (losses), **SV** (saves), **G** (games pitched), **GS** (games started), **IP** (innings pitched), **H** (hits allowed) and **HR** (home runs allowed). Next we have two statistics that are rates: **BB/9** (walks per nine innings) and **K/9** (strikeouts per nine innings), before returning to the unadjusted K (strikeouts).

Next up is **GB%** (ground ball percentage), which is the percentage of all batted balls that were hit on the ground, including both outs and hits. Remember, this is based on observational data and subject to human error, so please approach this with a healthy dose of skepticism.

BABIP (batting average on balls in play) is calculated using the same methodology as it is for position players, but it often tells us more about a pitcher than it does a hitter. With pitchers, a high BABIP is often due to poor defense or bad luck, and can often be an indicator of potential rebound, and a low BABIP may be cause to expect performance regression. (A typical league-average BABIP is close to .290-.300.)

The metrics **WHIP** (walks plus hits per inning pitched) and **ERA** (earned run average) are old standbys: WHIP measures walks and hits allowed on a per-inning basis, while ERA measures earned runs on a nine-inning basis. Neither of these stats are translated or adjusted.

DRA (Deserved Run Average) was described at length earlier, and measures how many runs the pitcher "deserved" to allow per nine innings. Please note that since we lack all the data points that would make for a "real" DRA for minor-league events, the DRA displayed for minor league partial-seasons is based off of different data. (That data is a modified version of our cFIP metric, which you can find more information about on our website.)

Just like with hitters, **WARP** (Wins Above Replacement Player) is a total value metric that puts pitchers of all stripes on the same scale as position players. We use DRA as the primary input for our calculation of WARP. You might notice that relief pitchers (due to their limited innings) may have a lower WARP than you were expecting or than you might see in other WARP-like metrics. WARP does not take leverage into account, just the actions a pitcher performs and the expected value of those actions…which ends up judging high-leverage relief pitchers differently than you might imagine given their prestige and market value.

MPH gives you the pitcher's 95th percentile velocity for the noted season, in order to give you an idea of what the *peak* fastball velocity a pitcher possesses. Since this comes from our pitch-tracking data, it is not publicly available for minor-league pitchers.

Finally, we display the three new pitching metrics we described earlier. **FB%** (fastball percentage) gives you the percentage of fastballs thrown out of all pitches. **WHF** (whiff rate) tells you the percentage of swinging strikes induced out of all pitches. **CSP** (called strike probability) expresses the likelihood of all pitches thrown to result in a called strike, after controlling for factors like handedness, umpire, pitch type, count and location.

PECOTA

All players have PECOTA projections for 2020, as well as a set of other numbers that describe the performance of comparable players according to PECOTA. All projections for 2020 are for the player at the date we went to press in early January and are projected into the league and park context as indicated by the team abbreviation. (Note that players at very low levels of the minors are too unpredictable to assess using these numbers.) All PECOTA projected statistics represent a player's projected major-league performance.

Below the projections are the player's three highest-scoring comparable players as determined by PECOTA. All comparables represent a snapshot of how the listed player was performing at the same age as the current player, so if a

23-year-old pitcher is compared to Bartolo Colón, he's actually being compared to a 23-year-old Colón, not the version that pitched for the Rangers in 2018, nor to Colón's career as a whole.

A few points about pitcher projections. First, we aren't yet projecting peak velocity, so that column will be blank in the PECOTA lines. Second, projecting DRA is trickier than evaluating past performance, because it is unclear how deserving each pitcher will be of his anticipated outcomes. However, we know that another DRA-related statistic–contextual FIP or cFIP-estimates future run scoring very well. So for PECOTA, the projected DRA figures you see are based on the past cFIPs generated by the pitcher and comparable players over time, along with the other factors described above.

Lineouts

In each chapter's Lineouts section, you'll find abbreviated text comments, as well as all the same information you'd find in our full player comments. The only difference is that we limit the stats boxes in this section to only including the 2019 information for each player.

Managers

After all those wonderful team chapters, we've got statistics for each big-league manager, all of whom are organized by alphabetical order. Here you'll find a block including an extraordinary amount of information collected from each manager's entire career. For more information on the acronyms and what they mean, please visit the Glossary at www.baseballprospectus.com.

There is one important metric that we'd like to call attention to, and you'll find it next to each manager's name: **wRM+** (weighted reliever management plus). Developed by Rob Arthur and Rian Watt, wRM+ investigates how good a manager is at using their best relievers during the moments of highest leverage, using both our proprietary DRA metric as well as Leverage Index. wRM+ is scaled to a league average of 100, and a wRM+ of 105 indicates that relievers were used approximately five percent "better" than average. On the other hand, a wRM+ of 95 would tell us the team used its relievers five percent "worse" than the average team.

While wRM+ does not have an extremely strong correlation with a manager, it is statistically significant; this means that a manager is not *entirely* responsible for a team's wRM+, but does have some effect on that number.

PECOTA Leaderboards

If you're familiar with PECOTA, then you'll have noticed that the projection system often appears bullish on players coming off a bad year and bearish on players coming off a good year. (This is because the system weights several previous seasons, not just the most recent one.) In addition, we publish the 50th

Minnesota Twins 2020

percentile projections for each player–which is smack in the middle of the range of projected production—which tends to mean PECOTA stat lines don't often have extreme results like 40 home runs or 250 strikeouts in a given season. In essence, PECOTA doesn't project very many extreme seasons.

At the end of the book, we've ranked the top players at each position based on their PECOTA projections. This might help you visualize just how a given player's projection compares to that of their peers, so that even if a dramatic stat line isn't projected, you can still imagine how they stack up against the rest of the league. ■

Part 1: Team Analysis

Minnesota Twins: Where Are You Going, Where Have You Been?

David Lesky, Keanan Lamb and Matthew Trueblood

2019: What Went Right
When the Cleveland Indians had a very quiet offseason prior to the 2019 campaign, the belief was that it wouldn't matter because there wasn't a challenger for the AL Central crown. PECOTA projected the Twins to finish a comfortable 15 or so games behind the Indians and take home a .500 record. So, for them to have won the division, and by the amount that they did, qualifies as something that went very right for an organization that hadn't finished atop the AL Central since 2010.

The offense was without a doubt what went *really* right for the Twins. They set a big-league record for home runs hit in a season, and they set it before the rosters even expanded. Yes, the caffeinated ball clearly helped some/many home runs reach their dinger destiny, but the Twins clubbing more than 300 balls over the fence and dusting the previous record of 267 was still an accomplishment. Five players hit 30 or more homers, eight players hit 20 or more and another, Marwin González, hit 15.

The best of the bunch was Nelson Cruz, the 38-year-old designated hitter. He hit .311/.392/.639 for a 152 DRC+ and clubbed 40 home runs for the fourth time in his career (and the first time since 2016) despite missing a quarter of the season. Catcher Mitch Garver, who came into the year with a career .259/.329/.405 line in 125 career games and had a career .428 SLG in the minors, turned on the power with a 30 home-run season despite only 93 games played. We might fantasize about how good our lives might be if everything simultaneously improved, but the Twins actually experienced what that might feel like. Max Kepler, Eddie Rosario, Jorge Polanco, Garver and Miguel Sanó all reached career highs in several or many categories, helping the Twins to score and score and keep on scoring. One of the most interesting positives came via the one breakthrough player who didn't hit many home runs, Luis Arráez. The 22-year old batsman handled second base, third base, shortstop and left field at various times, proving to be a valuable and versatile member of the team. He walked more than he struck out and seemed always to be getting on base. His presence allowed the Twins not to be over-reliant on Jonathan Schoop, whose chronic impatience limits his offensive upside.

You don't win 101 games without solid performances on the pitching side as well. José Berríos didn't quite take that next step to become a Cy Young candidate, but he was at least looking like he was on his way before a bit of a second-half slide. It was nevertheless a good year, with the pitcher reaching over 200 innings for the first time. The Twins figured out how to get the most out of Jake Odorizzi's added velocity, learning that five or six innings was usually enough before it was time to get him out of the game and go to a surprisingly deep, if unspectacular, bullpen.

Taylor Rogers took over the closer's role for himself and posted an impressive 8.2 strikeout-walk ratio (Justin Verlander, the qualified AL leader, finished at 7.1). Add in Trevor May, Tyler Duffey, and the trade-deadline acquisition of Sergio Romo, and the Twins bullpen recorded a 4.73 DRA, fifth-best in the AL. While the Twins didn't make the biggest moves at the deadline, they did act quickly to rebuild the bullpen with arms from the system as well as in trade, turning the unit into a strength by season's end.

2019: What Went Wrong

The Twins didn't win the most games in the American League, which led them to playing the Yankees in the ALDS. That's about as bad as it gets for the Twins. No team that wins 101 games wants their season to end as abruptly as Minnesota's did. In fact, they're the first team since the 1993 Giants to win 100+ games and not win a single game in the playoffs and the first 100-win team to make the playoffs and fail to win a game since the 1980 Yankees, so their dismissal was not your run of the mill LDS sweep.

Though it's hard to comprehend that much that went wrong for a 100-win team, there's no such thing as perfection and there were some issues. The Twins struggled to find quality starts throughout the season with only Berríos a generally consistent resource every fifth day. While Odorizzi was quite good, it probably would have been nice to get a few more innings from him on a start-to-start basis. Michael Pineda having his season cut short due to a PED suspension wasn't exactly what they were hoping for either (is it ever?), given that Martín Pérez regressed quickly after his fast start.

Injuries played a role as well. Byron Buxton was putting together the breakout year that everyone has been expecting for what seems like forever, but another injury put him on the shelf. It's fair to wonder if he's ever going to be healthy enough to be relied upon. Sam Dyson was brought in at the deadline to help shore up that bullpen, but his season-ending injury made him a dud for the Twins. —*David Lesky*

Prospect Outlook

You'll often see teams that make semi-surprising playoff runs mortgage the future by leveraging prospects for win-now players at the trade deadline. The Twins, however, held onto many of their prized assets and feature one of the deepest organizations in the game from top to bottom. Some are already contributing on the big-league roster, like **Brusdar Graterol**, while other former high picks like infielder **Nick Gordon** and OF/1B **Brent Rooker** are likely to debut early next year after solid Triple-A seasons.

Then there is the meat of the system: 2017 first overall pick **Royce Lewis**, who ascended into the upper minors despite so-so offensive production, is being featured at multiple positions in the Arizona Fall League and honing his approach. Lefty slugger **Alex Kiriloff** struggled with injuries to begin this year but caught fire in the final month and playoffs. He may also be knocking on the door for his call-up. Another high pick, **Trevor Larnach**, has been impressive, steady, and consistent in his pro career while developing his power stroke. If anything is lacking, it's that the system leans towards position players, yet right-handers **Jordan Balazovic** and **Jhoan Duran** took big steps in their development this season, finishing the year in Double-A.

The propensity to hit on high draft picks and J2 signees affords the Twins a rare ability to continuously restock the farm even with graduations and roster supplementing trades. Looking at every single Twins affiliate, you can find quality talent that rivals any collection of minor leaguers in baseball. —*Keanan Lamb*

2020 Outlook

Signing Josh Donaldson was the defining moment of the team's winter, and perhaps the best individual moment they've had in a decade. Donaldson is a fielding whiz at third base, and especially adept at going to his left to close the hole between his position and shortstop. That mitigates the negative effects of running Polanco out at short every day, and should help Minnesota's hurlers. In the process, the team keeps Sanó's bat in the lineup at all times, but shifts him to a position at which he should be much better.

The team will see offensive regression, too, not least because of the significant coaching losses they suffered when teams flocked toward the scent of Minnesota's highly successful 2019. Donaldson helps, offsetting some of the coming back to Earth we expect from (for instance) Mitch Garver. Meanwhile,

Garver will be spelled by a new backup and platoon partner, as Alex Avila signed a one-year deal to do just about everything just about the same way Jason Castro did it.

After being spurned in the pursuit of some bigger pitching fish, however, the Twins didn't do much to forestall regression from their hurlers. Odorizzi took the qualifying offer, and the team and Pineda reunited on a two-year deal, but it's hard to imagine the former outstripping the season he just had, and Pineda still has a quarter-season to serve on his suspension. Homer Bailey and Rich Hill were high-ceiling lottery tickets, but they weren't as cheap as those types of hurlers typically are. Hill's elbow rehab will keep him off the Target Field mound at least until mid-season. In addition to Odorizzi and Pineda, the team retained Sergio Romo, and they brought in Tyler Clippard to serve as the second lefty in their bullpen. (Clippard throws right-handed, but his splits make him a lefty from a strategic standpoint.)

As the winter progressed, it became clear that the Twins' starting depth was sufficient (even if they lacked anything like a true ace), and that their bullpen will be one of the best in baseball. Because of the former, the team preemptively shifted the flamethrowing Graterol to relief. Because of the latter, they were then willing to trade him to the Dodgers. In return, they got Kenta Maeda, and (in effect) short-circuited the market that had cut them out of the loop. Maeda is a much less expensive, but almost equally valuable, version of Zack Wheeler, Madison Bumgarner, Hyun-jin Ryu, or Dallas Keuchel. He becomes the team's co-ace, and does what little work was left in terms of shoring up the team's run prevention. With the AL's best lineup and a better pitching staff than most know, the Twins are now serious pennant contenders. —*Matthew Trueblood*

Performance Graphs

2019 Hit List Ranking

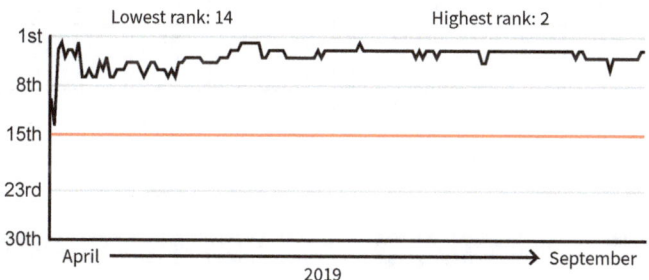

Committed Payroll (in millions)

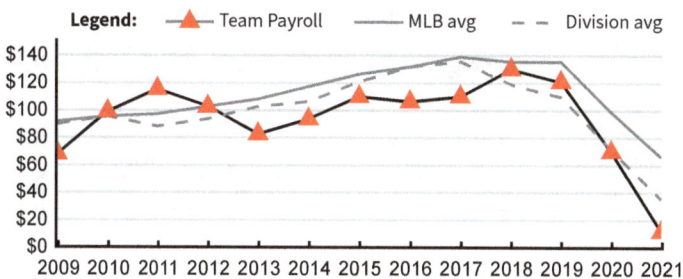

Farm System Ranking

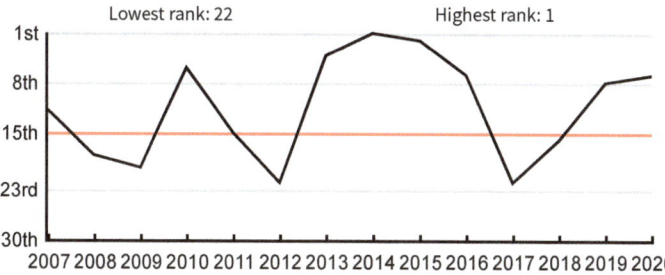

2019 Team Performance

ACTUAL STANDINGS

Team	W	L	Pct
MIN	**101**	**61**	**0.623**
CLE	93	69	0.574
CHA	72	89	0.447
KCA	59	103	0.364
DET	47	114	0.292

THIRD-ORDER STANDINGS

Team	W	L	Pct
MIN	**97**	**65**	**0.597**
CLE	87	75	0.535
CHA	66	95	0.412
KCA	59	103	0.364
DET	49	112	0.304

TOP HITTERS

Player	WARP
Jorge Polanco	5.3
Mitch Garver	4.4
Nelson Cruz	4.1

TOP PITCHERS

Player	WARP
José Berríos	2.9
Jake Odorizzi	2.7
Taylor Rogers	1.9

VITAL STATISTICS

Statistic Name	Value	Rank
Pythagenpat	.606	4th
Runs Scored per Game	5.80	2nd
Runs Allowed per Game	4.65	14th
Deserved Runs Created Plus	113	2nd
Deserved Run Average	4.94	18th
Fielding Independent Pitching	4.05	4th
Defensive Efficiency Rating	.691	25th
Batter Age	27.8	12th
Pitcher Age	27.9	14th
Salary	$119.7M	18th
Marginal $ per Marginal Win	$2.0M	28th
Injured List Days	819	5th
$ on IL	14%	14th

2020 Team Projections

PROJECTED STANDINGS

Team	W	L	Pct	+/-
MIN	**93.4**	**68.6**	**0.577**	**-8**
CLE	86.1	75.9	0.531	-7
CHA	82.5	79.5	0.509	10
DET	69.2	92.8	0.427	22
KCA	67.8	94.2	0.419	9

TOP PROJECTED HITTERS

Player	WARP
Miguel Sanó	3.9
Byron Buxton	3.4
Max Kepler	3.3

TOP PROJECTED PITCHERS

Player	WARP
Kenta Maeda	2.8
José Berríos	1.6
Michael Pineda	1.6

FARM SYSTEM REPORT

Top Prospect	Number of Top 101 Prospects
Royce Lewis, #21	4

KEY DEDUCTIONS

Player	WARP
Jonathan Schoop	2.0
C.J. Cron	1.6
Jason Castro	1.5
Kyle Gibson	0.5
Martín Pérez	0.1
Ryne Harper	0.1
Brusdar Graterol	-0.2
Stephen Gonsalves	-0.4
Kohl Stewart	-0.8

KEY ADDITIONS

Player	WARP
Josh Donaldson	3.0
Kenta Maeda	2.8
Michael Pineda	1.6
Alex Avila	0.7
Rich Hill	0.5
Tyler Clippard	0.4
Homer Bailey	0.4
Travis Blankenhorn	0.2
Gilberto Celestino	0.2
Jhoulys Chacín	0.2

Team Personnel

Executive Vice President, Chief Baseball Officer
Derek Falvey

Senior Vice President, General Manager
Thad Levine

Vice President, Assistant General Manager
Rob Antony

Vice President, Player Personnel
Mike Radcliff

Manager
Rocco Baldelli

BP Alumni
Ezra Wise

Target Field Stats

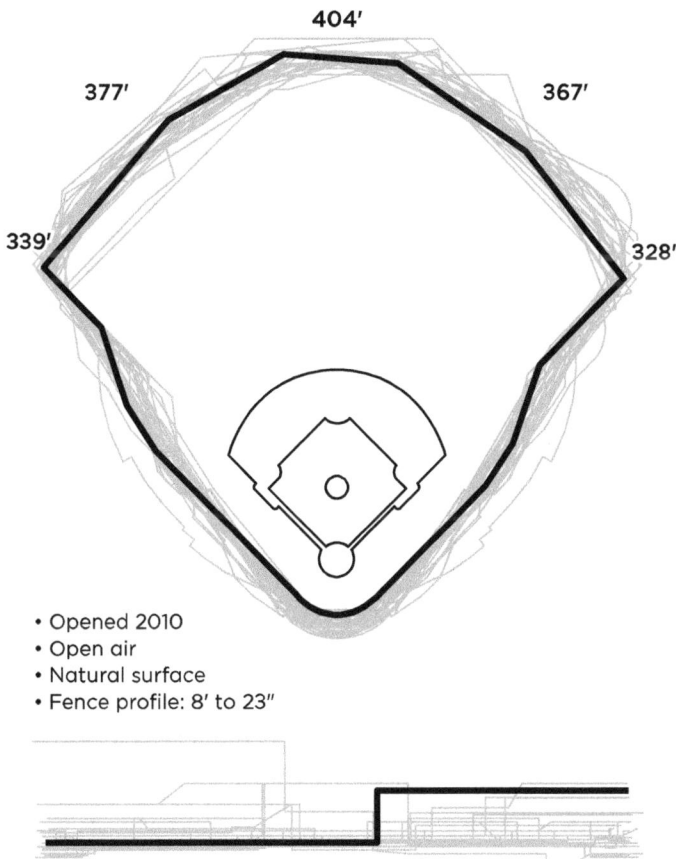

- Opened 2010
- Open air
- Natural surface
- Fence profile: 8' to 23"

Three-Year Park Factors

Runs	Runs/RH	Runs/LH	HR/RH	HR/LH
99	99	101	98	98

Twins Team Analysis

The 2019 Twins were the quintessential team for that season, in ways both very good and very bad. No single fact about the club better illustrates this than their home-run total, 307, which obliterated the old franchise and league records. On the other hand, and in the other valence, that home-run total was inflated by the aeroball, which permitted three other teams to hit what would also have been record-setting numbers of dingers, so it's hard to truly grasp what the record does and doesn't mean. The Twins were fun to watch, and in some senses, they were wildly successful: they won 101 games and cruised to the American League Central crown. After they were swept by the Yankees (yet again) in the Divisional Series, however, fans departed with a bitter taste in their mouths; the same sense of meaninglessness (perhaps even of artifice) that colored the home-run record settled over the team's won-lost record.

It's not just the aeroball distorting our understanding of the game as we embark on a new decade, however, and it's not only the Twins who were left buffeted by criss-crossing winds of change, and thus made to feel terrifyingly still, even as they make ample progress. The Statcast Era has had effects even more profound and far-reaching than most imagined when the system was first implemented in 2014. Off the big-league field and away from the Statcast cameras, other technological advancements have similarly thrown open new doors. A great many things we long believed to be fixed but largely unknowable have turned out to be knowable but highly fluid—from the aerodynamic properties of the baseball, to a player's individual talent level, to the interaction factors that make up a winning clubhouse.

That's set the game on its ear, and forced teams to adopt new philosophies based on a crucial premise: you have to work relentlessly to get ahead, but once there, you can't stop for even a moment. As teams prepare for 2020, the Twins exemplify that better than any other team.

Last year's Twins were not just a product of the aeroball. They were a team with talent in many places on the roster, and more importantly, they got more out of their talent than all but a few other teams in the majors. By replacing Paul Molitor (who was nobly open-minded about advanced information, given his age and background, but who wasn't the proactive conduit for that information the front office needed) with Rocco Baldelli, the team continued what was already an ongoing effort to better equip and develop their players. Baldelli and his coaching staff, led by bench coach Derek Shelton (who provided invaluable experience and organization to the man who beat him out for the job on the top step), altered everything about the way the Twins operated—even with regard to things that had already changed a lot over the previous seasons. Shelton quietly oversaw an increasingly aggressive array of defensive alignments, as the Twins stayed ahead of the sharply rising curve in shifts league-wide.

The front office hired Wes Johnson, a short guy from Arkansas who had spent the last decade instructing college pitchers and had never before held a job in pro ball, to be their pitching coach, making him the first person ever to make that jump directly. Under his tutelage, Trevor May and Tyler Duffey found the consistency and dominance that had long eluded them, taking the team's bullpen to a new level in the second half. They promoted advance scout Jeremy Hefner, an ex-pitcher in his early 30s, to assistant pitching coach, and Hefner helped implement informed changes that got multiple pitchers back on track at various points during the season.

They tethered emerging catcher Mitch Garver to catching coordinator Tanner Swanson, and Swanson reshaped Garver from a poor framer into an average-to-plus one. Meanwhile, the team's hitting infrastructure (which had been in place for a couple of years) found a new gear. If you want to find the secret of the Twins' success at the plate last year, don't look at the balls; look at the guys who flipped so many of them to Twins hitters. James Rowson and Rudy Hernandez had previously, though impermanently, fixed Byron Buxton and aided the impressive progress of Jorge Polanco and Max Kepler.

In 2019, they turned up the intensity, helping hitters find their optimal approaches, groove their swings to suit those approaches and consistently accomplish what the organization considered the most desirable outcome of a plate appearance: hard-hit balls, in the air, to the pull field. They even fixed Miguel Sanó on the fly, in the middle of the season, and helped him unlock his full power profile in the second half.

Meanwhile, organizational hitting coordinator Peter Fatse churned out players with the same focus and the same consistent success in the minor leagues. The Twins hit the ball hard, in the air, to the pull field, in 5.5 percent of their plate appearances; the league-average rate was 4 percent, and no team other than the Twins reached 5 percent. The A's, who were second-best at it, were as far behind the Twins as they were ahead of the 13th-place Orioles.

All that success couldn't go unnoticed, however, and even if the Twins were a half-step ahead in some aspects, the whole league is now immersed in similarly cooperative coaching and development superstructures. Right after the Twins' unceremonious playoff ouster, they fell victim to a shockingly rapid brain drain among the team's most well-known development people. Swanson and Fatse got jobs on the big-league coaching staffs of the Yankees and Red Sox, respectively; Rowson became the bench coach and offensive coordinator (title inflation is a trend more pervasive than heavy slider usage) for the Marlins;

Hefner left for the Mets' pitching coach job; and Shelton was hired as the Pirates' new manager. That's enough to stagger a team, especially one that depended so much on the synergy between front office, field staff and players.

Pushing to stay ahead despite their losses, the Twins hired (if anything) even more aggressively. They coaxed Mike Bell, who had spent over a decade in the player-development department for the Diamondbacks, into replacing Shelton as the bench coach. They lured Tucker Frawley, the mastermind of recruitment, player development and strategy for Yale's program, into becoming their assistant field coordinator and coordinator of skill development. And they shelled out top dollar (for the position) to replace Fatse with Donegal Fergus, a highly-regarded collegiate hitting guru from the University of California, Santa Barbara.

On top of on-field, player development-focused hires, Minnesota hired Chris Mitchell, formerly of FanGraphs and the architect of a projection system for minor-league players, to join a front office that has been built out in ways that even a few years ago would have been unimaginable to any Twins fan. The team hired Daniel Adler to head their research and development department in late 2017, and ever since, they've been snatching up impressive and improbable talents to help them generate and manage as much useful information as possible. They've brought everyone from former Baseball-Reference.com developer Hans Van Slooten to PITCHf/x analyst-turned-Rays executive Josh Kalk to Baseball America head honcho John Manuel into their fold, stretching tendrils deep into the internet baseball community to find people with valuable perspectives, skills and relationships. There's some risk that the brain drain has become a money pit, but the team is still convinced it can spend both money and intellectual resources in ways that will augment their present and future ability to find and maximize talent.

How much of that work must they do, from moment to moment, as opposed to being able to count on the baseline levels of the players they've acquired? How much can players improve even without the organization's direct help, the way Jake Odorizzi did in 2019? After a winter at the Florida Baseball Ranch, Odorizzi had the breakout that multiple organizations had hoped to eventually extract from him. He was more mechanically efficient, leading to more velocity and more life on his stuff. He was more confident and consistent in using his full repertoire, locating to each quadrant of the strike zone and inducing opponents to expand that zone. Johnson was a positive influence, but Odorizzi largely remade himself, and that's not uncommon in today's game. The trick is for teams to allow players to pursue options like the Ranch, outside their direct control, and to communicate openly and honestly enough to ensure players can get the full benefit from those options.

Odorizzi will be back in 2020, but it's no guarantee that all his improvements will hold, as the league adjusts to his new arsenal and style and forces him to adjust back.

On a team level, similar balancing acts are necessary, but they're trickier. The team can't abandon what it has done well, but must keep adapting and anticipating changes in trends and opponent strategies. After a disappointing 2018 in which they considered their clubhouse culture part of the problem, they assembled a perfect blend of personalities and backgrounds in 2019, with players and coaches working (mostly) harmoniously and teammates finding numerous ways to support and reinforce one another's success. Baldelli managed the depth the front office gave him with the savvy and deftness of a more veteran skipper. Reproducing that magic in 2020, however, will be hard, not only because of the coaching turnover, but because even the players and coaches in the room will be one year different, with different expectations, different ideas and different senses of their relative statuses.

The baseball itself is no more predictable. The league's self-investigation yielded few satisfying conclusions or plans of action, so it's unlikely big changes in the liveliness of the ball are forthcoming, but as we've seen, even small changes can have big consequences. That's the short version of much longer stories in many other aspects of baseball right now, and it's the scariest thing for Twins fans to ponder as a new season looms. The Twins haven't undergone small changes, but big ones, and the consequences of those could turn them back toward the middle of the pack, or catapult them into the class of the American League's elite.

In either case, Twins fans won't consider that much has changed unless one crucial thing does: Minnesota needs to win a playoff series. That can't happen until they win a whole lot of regular-season games again, and the front office's dedication to acquiring and preparing players who can do that is exciting and interesting.

But for all their data and technology-informed technique improvements—and for all of their redefinition and trailblazing in coaching, development and front-office hires—there's one thing these Twins can't reliably change: the dynamic of October.

—Matt Trueblood is an author of Baseball Prospectus.

Part 2: Player Analysis

Minnesota Twins 2020

PLAYER COMMENTS WITH GRAPHS

Ehire Adrianza   INF
Born: 08/21/89   Age: 30   Bats: B   Throws: R
Height: 6'1"   Weight: 195   Origin: International Free Agent, 2006

YEAR	TEAM	LVL	AGE	PA	R	2B	3B	HR	RBI	BB	K	SB	CS	AVG/OBP/SLG
2017	ROC	AAA	27	44	1	0	0	0	3	6	11	0	1	.216/.326/.216
2017	MIN	MLB	27	186	30	9	2	2	24	16	25	8	1	.265/.324/.383
2018	MIN	MLB	28	366	42	23	1	6	39	24	82	5	1	.251/.301/.379
2019	MIN	MLB	29	236	34	8	3	5	22	20	40	0	2	.272/.349/.416
2020	MIN	MLB	30	315	31	13	1	7	32	24	60	6	2	.238/.306/.364

Comparables: Didi Gregorius, Stephen Drew, Andre Rodgers

Pitchers gifted Adrianza first-pitch balls at an abnormal rate, and a season after lifting and separating a little too often, he rediscovered his approach, found the opposite field and put together the first league-average offensive effort of his career. He did it at a career-high six different positions, too, as he added right field reps for the first time. He's creeping into his 30s now and he'll get a little pricey for the role in this, his fourth and final year of arbitration, so he's going to have to fight for his right to party with the 26-man Twins at every step of the way in 2020.

YEAR	TEAM	LVL	AGE	PA	DRC+	VORP	BABIP	BRR	FRAA	WARP
2017	ROC	AAA	27	44	72	-1.6	.308	-0.1	LF(4): 1.0, SS(2): 0.3	0.1
2017	MIN	MLB	27	186	87	6.5	.291	1.6	SS(29): 3.0, LF(17): 1.5	1.1
2018	MIN	MLB	28	366	82	7.4	.313	0.7	SS(64): -6.1, 3B(28): 0.6	0.0
2019	MIN	MLB	29	236	101	8.2	.311	-1.2	SS(24): 1.4, 3B(24): 0.0	0.8
2020	MIN	MLB	30	315	79	0.3	.279	0.0	1B -1, 2B 0	0.0

Ehire Adrianza, continued

Batted Ball Distribution

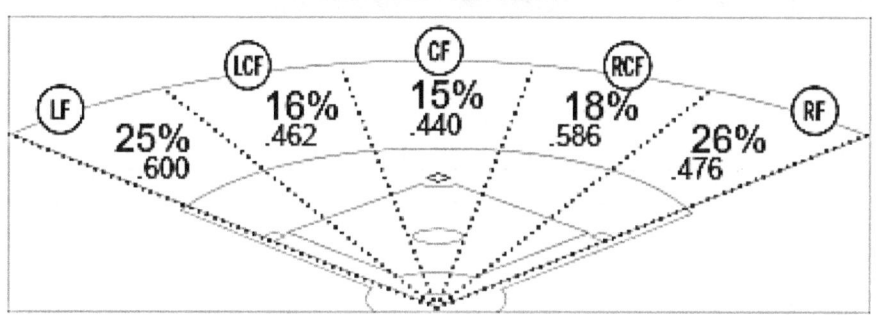

Strike Zone vs LHP **Strike Zone vs RHP**

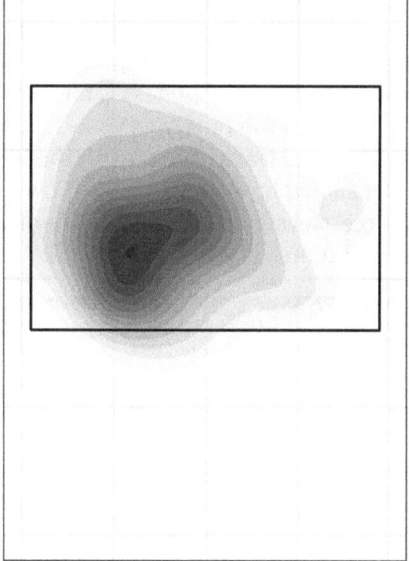

Minnesota Twins 2020

Luis Arraez 2B

Born: 04/09/97   Age: 23   Bats: L   Throws: R
Height: 5'10"   Weight: 177   Origin: International Free Agent, 2013

YEAR	TEAM	LVL	AGE	PA	R	2B	3B	HR	RBI	BB	K	SB	CS	AVG/OBP/SLG
2018	FTM	A+	21	258	27	14	3	1	20	19	28	2	3	.320/.373/.421
2018	CHT	AA	21	195	25	6	0	2	16	13	16	2	0	.298/.345/.365
2019	PEN	AA	22	164	18	6	1	0	14	18	13	3	3	.342/.415/.397
2019	ROC	AAA	22	73	8	4	0	0	8	6	2	1	0	.348/.397/.409
2019	MIN	MLB	22	366	54	20	1	4	28	36	29	2	2	.334/.399/.439
2020	MIN	MLB	23	525	52	26	2	6	50	41	52	3	1	.303/.360/.397

Comparables: Abiatal Avelino, Odúbel Herrera, L.J. Hoes

"Taking an enemy on the battlefield is like a hawk taking a bird," Ghost Dog once said, "even though it enters into the midst of a thousand of them, it gives no attention to any bird other than the one that it has first marked." Watching Arraez shuffle and shake his head at a diving slider off the black, you get the sense he has that kind of monomaniacal focus. An impeccable eye and a samurai-worthy stroke propelled Arraez to the third-best batting average in baseball (minimum 300 at-bats), and he did that on the back of the best contact rate in the game. Emptiness is form; Arraez's bat shape-shifts to find pitches in all corners of the zone, and while he doesn't drive the ball against lefties, he sees 'em and leaves 'em plenty. The leather must come into accord with its own, but it should have its chance to grow over a full season of regular starts in 2020. A successful sequel would mean finding his Way into the starting nine for a long time to come.

YEAR	TEAM	LVL	AGE	PA	DRC+	VORP	BABIP	BRR	FRAA	WARP
2018	FTM	A+	21	258	134	14.2	.356	-2.4	2B(40): 1.7, 3B(6): 0.3	1.6
2018	CHT	AA	21	195	112	6.2	.315	0.0	2B(27): -1.0, 3B(10): 0.3	0.9
2019	PEN	AA	22	164	177	11.8	.376	-0.9	2B(15): -0.1, 3B(15): 4.2	2.2
2019	ROC	AAA	22	73	130	3.5	.354	-0.9	SS(8): 0.4, 2B(4): 1.5	0.6
2019	MIN	MLB	22	366	122	22.6	.355	2.9	2B(49): -2.8, LF(21): 1.5	2.3
2020	MIN	MLB	23	525	103	25.4	.331	2.5	2B -1, 3B 0	2.5

Luis Arraez, continued

Batted Ball Distribution

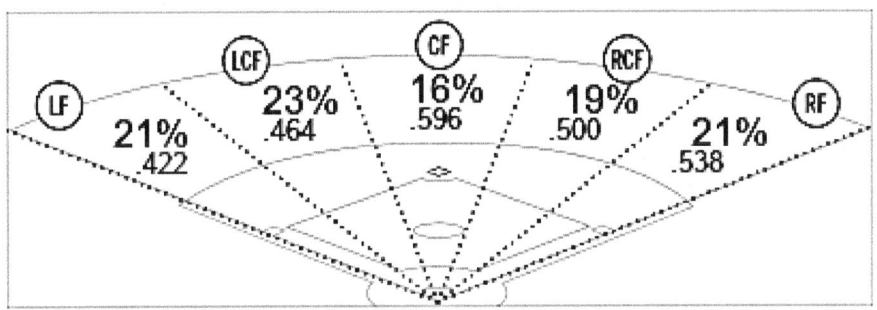

Strike Zone vs LHP   **Strike Zone vs RHP**

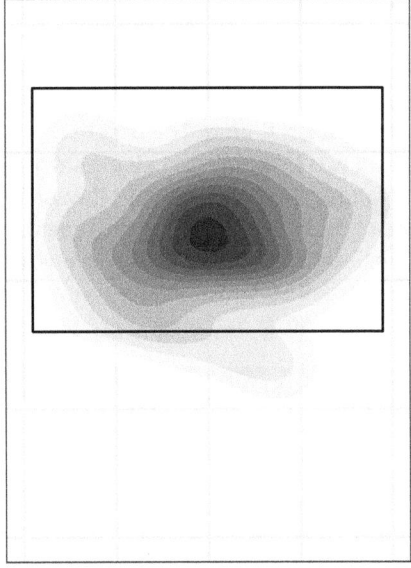

Minnesota Twins 2020

Willians Astudillo C
Born: 10/14/91 Age: 28 Bats: R Throws: R
Height: 5'9" Weight: 225 Origin: International Free Agent, 2008

YEAR	TEAM	LVL	AGE	PA	R	2B	3B	HR	RBI	BB	K	SB	CS	AVG/OBP/SLG
2017	RNO	AAA	25	128	22	14	0	4	22	4	5	0	1	.342/.370/.558
2018	ROC	AAA	26	307	30	17	1	12	38	10	14	7	4	.276/.314/.469
2018	MIN	MLB	26	97	9	4	1	3	21	2	3	0	0	.355/.371/.516
2019	ROC	AAA	27	83	18	1	0	5	19	2	2	1	1	.423/.446/.628
2019	MIN	MLB	27	204	28	9	0	4	21	5	8	0	0	.268/.299/.379
2020	MIN	MLB	28	245	27	12	0	8	31	7	15	1	1	.279/.315/.442

Comparables: Ildemaro Vargas, Charles Silvera, Brayan Peña

To have loved and lost, or to have never loved at all? The poetry and prose of Astudillo's game turned sour in 2019, as inconsistent opportunity and an inability to replicate his magical production of 2018 conspired to drop the big man down to Triple-A before an oblique injury scuttled his efforts at a rebound. The baseball world was fortunate to catch a stray glimpse of his wonder after rosters expanded in September, but it wasn't enough to salvage his season. Tortugas are of course slow and steady types blessed with a steadfast persistence. All hope is not lost, then, that he plows on ahead and blossoms into a utility stalwart. We stand with just about every corner of the baseball-loving world in hoping for that outcome.

YEAR	TEAM	P. COUNT	FRM RUNS	BLK RUNS	THRW RUNS	TOT RUNS
2017	RNO	2571	1.4	0.0	-0.2	1.0
2018	MIN	2234	1.1	0.5	0.0	1.6
2018	ROC	5149	1.4	0.3	0.3	1.6
2019	MIN	2577	-0.3	0.0	-0.1	-0.4
2019	ROC	1130	1.5	0.0	0.0	1.4
2020	MIN	2526	0.6	0.0	-0.1	0.5

YEAR	TEAM	LVL	AGE	PA	DRC+	VORP	BABIP	BRR	FRAA	WARP
2017	RNO	AAA	25	128	124	7.8	.330	-1.4	C(19): 0.9, 3B(14): 0.0	0.9
2018	ROC	AAA	26	307	110	16.0	.255	-1.4	C(39): 2.5, 3B(28): 0.6	1.7
2018	MIN	MLB	26	97	129	8.4	.341	0.4	C(16): 2.1, 3B(6): 0.0	1.0
2019	ROC	AAA	27	83	169	14.2	.389	0.6	C(8): 1.3, 3B(5): 0.4	1.1
2019	MIN	MLB	27	204	95	6.2	.258	-2.1	C(21): -0.4, 1B(15): -0.3	0.4
2020	MIN	MLB	28	245	100	6.4	.270	-0.7	1B 0, C 1	0.6

Willians Astudillo, continued

Batted Ball Distribution

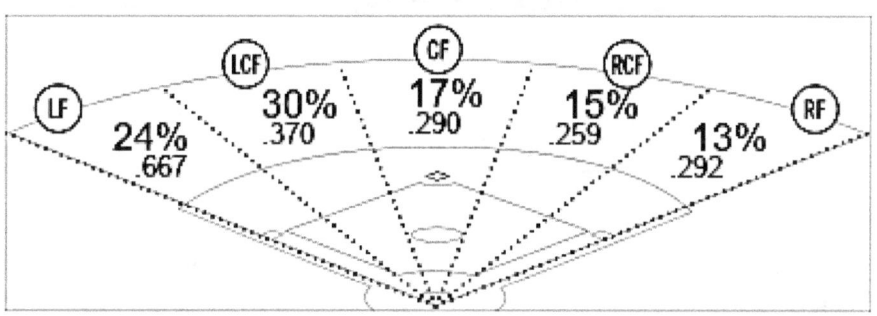

Strike Zone vs LHP   Strike Zone vs RHP

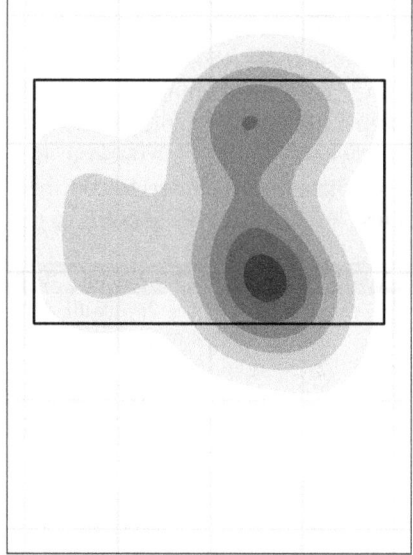

Minnesota Twins 2020

Alex Avila C

Born: 01/29/87 Age: 33 Bats: L Throws: R
Height: 5'11" Weight: 210 Origin: Round 5, 2008 Draft (#163 overall)

YEAR	TEAM	LVL	AGE	PA	R	2B	3B	HR	RBI	BB	K	SB	CS	AVG/OBP/SLG
2017	DET	MLB	30	264	30	11	0	11	32	43	80	0	1	.274/.394/.475
2017	CHN	MLB	30	112	11	2	1	3	17	19	40	0	0	.239/.369/.380
2018	ARI	MLB	31	234	13	6	0	7	20	37	90	0	0	.165/.299/.304
2019	ARI	MLB	32	201	22	8	0	9	24	36	68	1	0	.207/.353/.421
2020	MIN	MLB	33	245	29	9	0	8	28	41	88	1	0	.218/.352/.380

Comparables: Jason Castro, Ron Karkovice, Geovany Soto

The list of pitchers Avila has caught is a Who's Who list of All-Star and Cy Young-caliber talent. Justin Verlander, Max Scherzer, David Price, Chris Sale, Jon Lester, Jake Arrieta and Zack Greinke all dot the veteran backstop's ledger. (Fine, we can throw Rick Porcello in there, too. He *did* win a Cy Young once). Avila's longevity in the league can mostly be attributed to the fact that pitchers seem to enjoy throwing to him, and while he's declined to the point where "serviceable backup" is his most ideal role, he's competent enough at the plate (for a catcher) to continue being worth rostering even if teams more or less know what they're going to get at this point.

YEAR	TEAM	P. COUNT	FRM RUNS	BLK RUNS	THRW RUNS	TOT RUNS
2017	DET	6716	-5.8	0.7	0.2	-4.8
2017	CHN	3507	-3.3	-0.2	0.0	-3.2
2018	ARI	7984	3.7	0.3	0.0	4.3
2019	ARI	7089	-0.1	2.3	0.7	2.8
2020	MIN	9345	-4.8	0.5	1.1	-3.2

YEAR	TEAM	LVL	AGE	PA	DRC+	VORP	BABIP	BRR	FRAA	WARP
2017	DET	MLB	30	264	107	16.6	.380	-1.5	C(50): -0.5, 1B(16): -0.9	1.0
2017	CHN	MLB	30	112	107	5.6	.388	0.5	C(28): 0.2, 1B(3): 0.2	0.7
2018	ARI	MLB	31	234	62	-0.1	.253	-1.4	C(61): 3.2, 1B(3): 0.0	0.2
2019	ARI	MLB	32	201	96	9.4	.287	-1.1	C(54): 2.1, P(2): 0.0	1.0
2020	MIN	MLB	33	245	101	10.0	.342	-0.8	C -4	0.6

Alex Avila, continued

Batted Ball Distribution

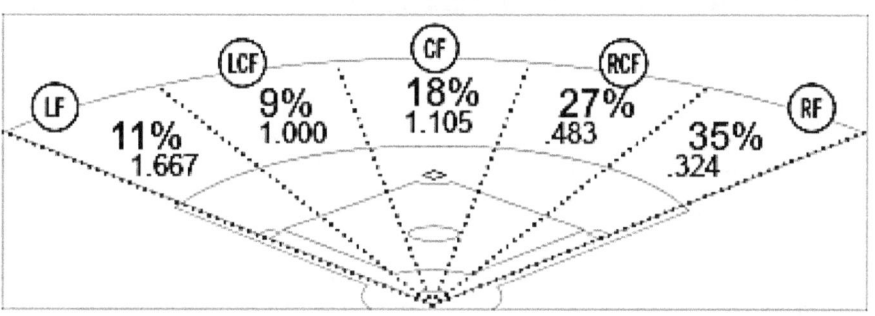

Strike Zone vs LHP   **Strike Zone vs RHP**

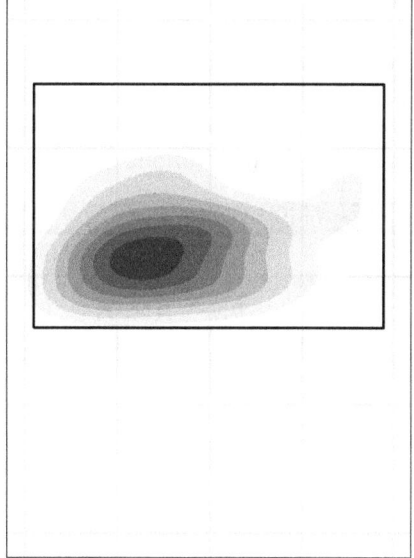

Byron Buxton   CF

Born: 12/18/93   Age: 26   Bats: R   Throws: R
Height: 6'2"   Weight: 190   Origin: Round 1, 2012 Draft (#2 overall)

YEAR	TEAM	LVL	AGE	PA	R	2B	3B	HR	RBI	BB	K	SB	CS	AVG/OBP/SLG
2017	MIN	MLB	23	511	69	14	6	16	51	38	150	29	1	.253/.314/.413
2018	ROC	AAA	24	148	22	11	1	4	14	9	42	4	1	.272/.331/.456
2018	MIN	MLB	24	94	8	4	0	0	4	3	28	5	0	.156/.183/.200
2019	MIN	MLB	25	295	48	30	4	10	46	19	68	14	3	.262/.314/.513
2020	MIN	MLB	26	490	52	23	6	18	60	34	131	15	3	.223/.283/.419

Comparables: Cameron Maybin, Wil Myers, Clint Frazier

Buxton was doing it—he was doing *it*!—and then he met a familiar foe: the injury bug. There are few more electrifying players on the planet than a healthy Buxton, an impeccable athletic marvel on the field who streaks over grass and dirt alike with a churn that would make Karl Gustaf Patrik de Laval blush. But his all-out style of play giveth, and it taketh away. He was concussed on a diving catch, then had his campaign halted prematurely when he underwent shoulder surgery—the kind that entails a half-year of rehab. His cost control and talent capture the Twins in an awkward spot, and there are just a whole bunch of parallel universes where his career shakes out a whole bunch of different ways from here. The Twins exist only in this one, wherein Buxton seems cursed to perpetual disappointment.

YEAR	TEAM	LVL	AGE	PA	DRC+	VORP	BABIP	BRR	FRAA	WARP
2017	MIN	MLB	23	511	86	17.6	.339	7.4	CF(137): 25.4	4.2
2018	ROC	AAA	24	148	103	8.8	.367	1.4	CF(28): 9.0	1.5
2018	MIN	MLB	24	94	57	-7.6	.226	0.3	CF(27): 1.4	0.0
2019	MIN	MLB	25	295	99	10.6	.314	4.4	CF(86): 14.2	2.9
2020	MIN	MLB	26	490	81	9.6	.274	3.4	CF 20	3.1

Byron Buxton, continued

Batted Ball Distribution

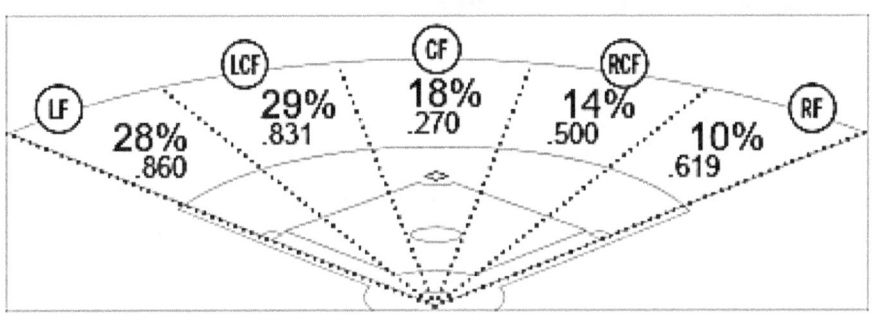

Strike Zone vs LHP   Strike Zone vs RHP

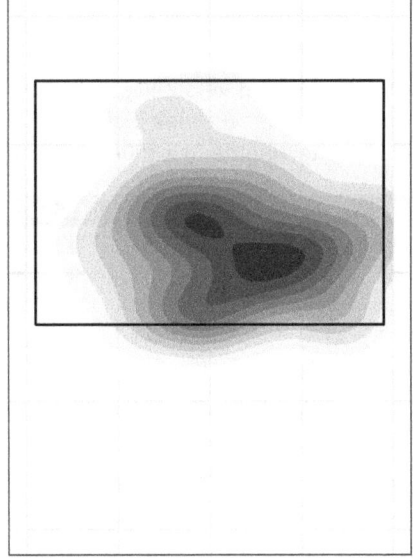

Minnesota Twins 2020

Jake Cave OF
Born: 12/04/92   Age: 27   Bats: L   Throws: L
Height: 6'0"   Weight: 200   Origin: Round 6, 2011 Draft (#209 overall)

YEAR	TEAM	LVL	AGE	PA	R	2B	3B	HR	RBI	BB	K	SB	CS	AVG/OBP/SLG
2017	TRN	AA	24	140	19	13	2	5	18	10	33	1	0	.266/.317/.516
2017	SWB	AAA	24	297	47	13	3	15	38	18	82	1	3	.324/.367/.554
2018	ROC	AAA	25	250	26	9	1	6	28	26	55	4	2	.269/.352/.403
2018	MIN	MLB	25	309	54	16	2	13	45	18	102	2	1	.265/.313/.473
2019	ROC	AAA	26	214	37	18	4	7	39	15	50	5	0	.352/.393/.592
2019	MIN	MLB	26	228	28	11	2	8	25	21	71	0	0	.258/.351/.455
2020	MIN	MLB	27	245	26	11	2	7	29	18	74	2	1	.245/.307/.410

Comparables: Duke Snider, Peter Bourjos, Tyler Austin

Cave continues to occupy that awkward space between being a fourth outfielder and being an up-and-down player. He scuffled out of the gate last season, suggesting he was unlikely to replicate his pleasant freshman efforts. His woes were such that he even found himself back in Triple-A in mid-May, the first in a series of demotions and recalls. From that point forward, Cave hit well enough to raise his numbers (relative to the league) close to what he produced the year prior. His versatility and sure-fine-adequate array of skills should allow him to continue receiving big-league at-bats. Cave's performance in 2020 will help dictate whether it's 300-plus annually, or something closer to half that.

YEAR	TEAM	LVL	AGE	PA	DRC+	VORP	BABIP	BRR	FRAA	WARP
2017	TRN	AA	24	140	113	6.3	.319	-1.0	LF(17): 0.7, CF(7): -0.5	0.5
2017	SWB	AAA	24	297	150	25.2	.414	0.5	CF(30): -1.8, RF(25): 2.2	2.2
2018	ROC	AAA	25	250	115	12.9	.327	-0.1	RF(36): 5.4, CF(17): -0.6	1.6
2018	MIN	MLB	25	309	93	18.0	.363	3.1	CF(70): -7.5, RF(11): 0.3	0.3
2019	ROC	AAA	26	214	141	21.6	.437	1.1	CF(36): -3.5, RF(7): -0.8	1.3
2019	MIN	MLB	26	228	89	3.2	.358	1.3	RF(45): -1.7, CF(23): 0.2	0.3
2020	MIN	MLB	27	245	89	4.6	.332	1.3	RF 1, CF -1	0.4

Jake Cave, continued

Batted Ball Distribution

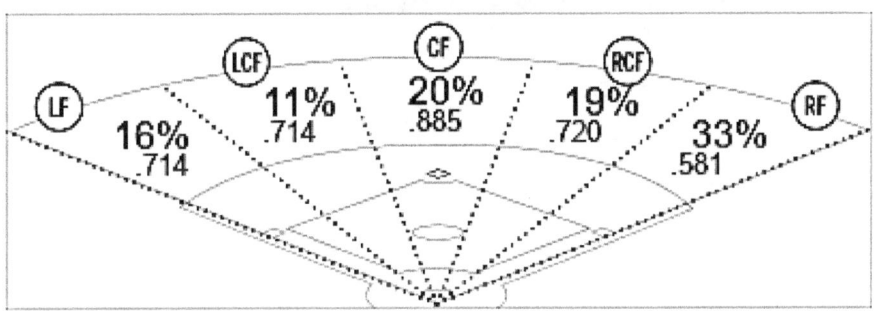

Strike Zone vs LHP

Strike Zone vs RHP

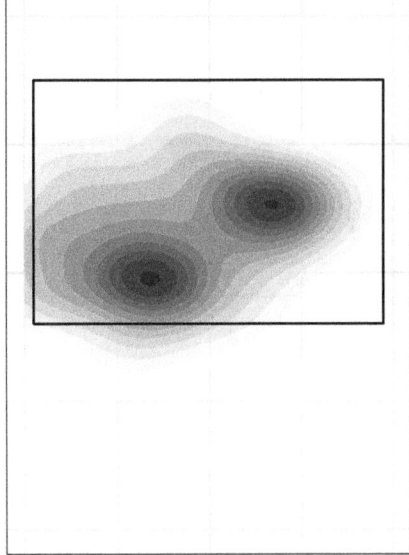

Nelson Cruz DH

Born: 07/01/80   Age: 39   Bats: R   Throws: R
Height: 6'2"   Weight: 230   Origin: International Free Agent, 1998

YEAR	TEAM	LVL	AGE	PA	R	2B	3B	HR	RBI	BB	K	SB	CS	AVG/OBP/SLG
2017	SEA	MLB	36	645	91	28	0	39	119	70	140	1	1	.288/.375/.549
2018	SEA	MLB	37	591	70	18	1	37	97	55	122	1	0	.256/.342/.509
2019	MIN	MLB	38	521	81	26	0	41	108	56	131	0	1	.311/.392/.639
2020	MIN	MLB	40	560	84	26	1	38	99	54	148	2	1	.279/.358/.561

Comparables: Manny Ramirez, Shin-Soo Choo, Donn Clendenon

Sure, Cruz was worth four wins (as a designated hitter!) and barreled balls at a higher rate than anyone else while anchoring the best homer-hitting team in baseball history...but have you seen him hit a golf ball? Somehow, Cruz's signature moment came well after the season ended, when he went viral for teeing off. While he can't be more than a couple years away from hitting the links more often, he has yet to show signs of mortality—save for, perhaps, a torn wrist tendon that cost him chunks of last season. Cruz will try for an encore performance in 2020 as part of a painfully team-friendly deal. The 40-year-old designated hitter is not a player type that tends to inspire confidence—Cruz is, safely, the exception.

YEAR	TEAM	LVL	AGE	PA	DRC+	VORP	BABIP	BRR	FRAA	WARP
2017	SEA	MLB	36	645	143	40.1	.315	-1.8	RF(5): -0.1	4.2
2018	SEA	MLB	37	591	132	27.5	.264	-1.2	RF(4): 0.1	3.1
2019	MIN	MLB	38	521	152	43.5	.351	-1.0		4.1
2020	MIN	MLB	40	560	139	27.8	.323	-1.0	RF -1	2.8

Nelson Cruz, continued

Batted Ball Distribution

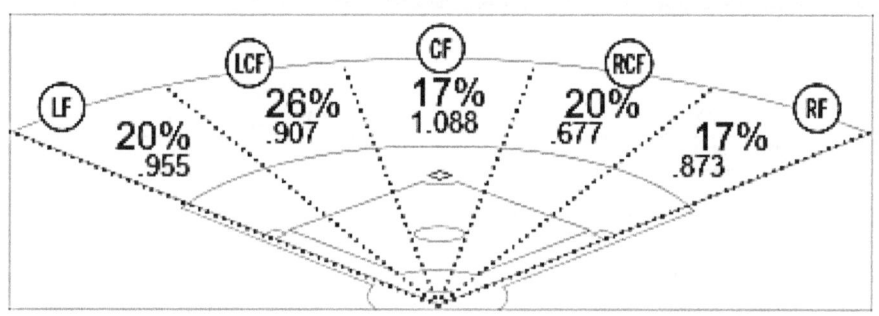

Strike Zone vs LHP **Strike Zone vs RHP**

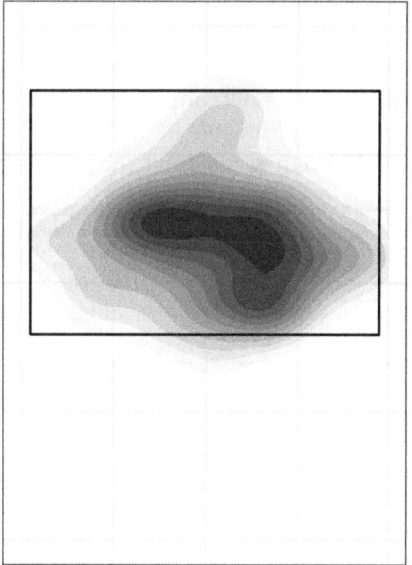

Minnesota Twins 2020

Josh Donaldson 3B

Born: 12/08/85   Age: 34   Bats: R   Throws: R
Height: 6'1"   Weight: 210   Origin: Round 1, 2007 Draft (#48 overall)

YEAR	TEAM	LVL	AGE	PA	R	2B	3B	HR	RBI	BB	K	SB	CS	AVG/OBP/SLG
2017	TOR	MLB	31	496	65	21	0	33	78	76	111	2	2	.270/.385/.559
2018	TOR	MLB	32	159	22	11	0	5	16	21	44	2	0	.234/.333/.423
2018	CLE	MLB	32	60	8	3	0	3	7	10	10	0	0	.280/.400/.520
2019	ATL	MLB	33	659	96	33	0	37	94	100	155	4	2	.259/.379/.521
2020	ATL	MLB	34	600	83	26	1	31	90	85	145	5	1	.249/.364/.490

Comparables: Todd Frazier, José Bautista, Howard Johnson

In the immediate aftermath of signing a one-year deal with the Braves for the 2019 season, Donaldson told anybody who doubted bringing him into the fold to look at the back of his baseball card. It would all come down to whether or not the former AL MVP could stay on the field and the Bringer of Rain answered that completely, playing in 155 games for the first time since 2016. It wasn't quite the OBP or slugging of his peak, but Donaldson certainly reminded everyone why he could have enough audacity to cite the credentials of his peak as enough reason to bet on himself. The torrential downpours from the 34-year-old, however, only came in the friendly confines of SunTrust Park—his 1.037 OPS there far eclipsing his .785 OPS on the road. Guess it's a good thing for Donaldson they still don't show splits on the back of a baseball card.

YEAR	TEAM	LVL	AGE	PA	DRC+	VORP	BABIP	BRR	FRAA	WARP
2017	TOR	MLB	31	496	141	44.8	.289	1.3	3B(105): -5.9, SS(4): -0.2	3.8
2018	TOR	MLB	32	159	106	4.1	.303	-0.4	3B(26): -0.9, 1B(1): 0.1	0.5
2018	CLE	MLB	32	60	106	3.5	.297	-0.8	3B(12): -0.9	0.1
2019	ATL	MLB	33	659	130	51.6	.292	-1.0	3B(148): 1.2	5.1
2020	ATL	MLB	34	600	124	16.1	.287	-0.2	3B -1, SS 0	3.9

Josh Donaldson, continued

Batted Ball Distribution

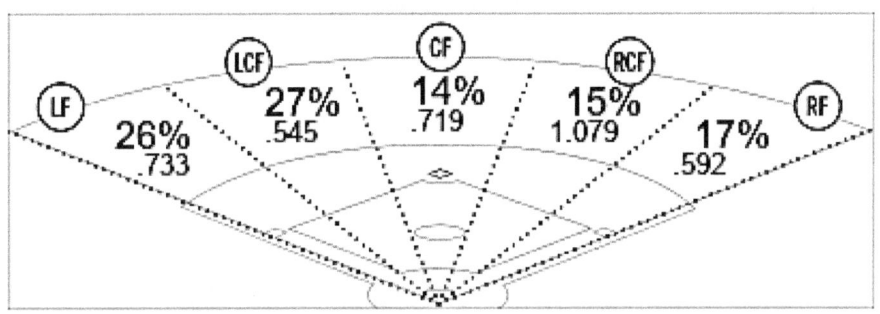

Strike Zone vs LHP   **Strike Zone vs RHP**

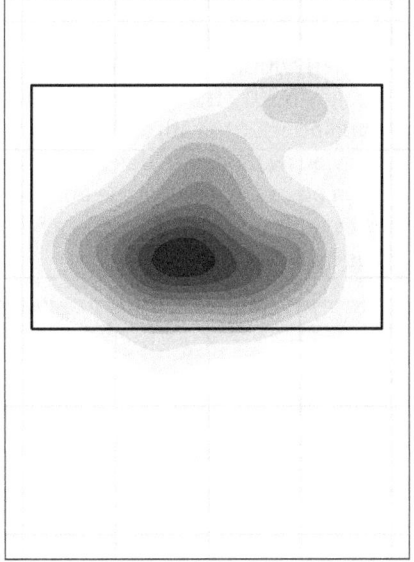

Mitch Garver C

Born: 01/15/91   Age: 29   Bats: R   Throws: R
Height: 6'1"   Weight: 220   Origin: Round 9, 2013 Draft (#260 overall)

YEAR	TEAM	LVL	AGE	PA	R	2B	3B	HR	RBI	BB	K	SB	CS	AVG/OBP/SLG
2017	ROC	AAA	26	372	56	29	0	17	45	50	85	2	0	.291/.387/.541
2017	MIN	MLB	26	52	5	1	3	0	3	6	15	0	0	.196/.288/.348
2018	MIN	MLB	27	335	38	19	2	7	45	29	72	0	0	.268/.335/.414
2019	MIN	MLB	28	359	70	16	1	31	67	41	87	0	0	.273/.365/.630
2020	MIN	MLB	29	455	60	21	1	25	70	46	115	0	0	.244/.329/.489

Comparables: Jorge Posada, Kelly Shoppach, Yan Gomes

If there's one theme to this chapter, it's that of players improving after working with the Twins' new coaches to alter their approach. No player reaped greater rewards in 2019 than Garver. His offensive potential intrigued scouts in the minors, particularly during a stellar Triple-A

YEAR	TEAM	P. COUNT	FRM RUNS	BLK RUNS	THRW RUNS	TOT RUNS
2017	MIN	832	-0.9	-0.1	0.0	-1.0
2017	ROC	8976	3.3	-0.9	0.4	2.5
2018	MIN	11726	-8.2	0.2	-0.4	-8.5
2019	MIN	10997	4.2	-0.3	-0.4	3.3
2020	MIN	15381	-7.0	-0.8	-1.2	-9.0

campaign in 2017 that pushed him into the bigs, and he atoned for a disappointing 2018 with a barrage of walks and home runs. Just as impressively, his previously mediocre defense took a step forward, as he learned to better settle in place and control the bottom of the zone. A year remains before Garver reaches arbitration, making him a bigger steal for the club than all those extra strikes he found last season.

YEAR	TEAM	LVL	AGE	PA	DRC+	VORP	BABIP	BRR	FRAA	WARP
2017	ROC	AAA	26	372	165	39.4	.347	0.2	C(67): 3.6, LF(14): 0.9	4.4
2017	MIN	MLB	26	52	71	-1.0	.290	0.2	C(13): -1.1, 1B(3): 0.3	-0.1
2018	MIN	MLB	27	335	100	14.1	.330	-1.3	C(86): -8.5, 1B(5): -0.1	0.5
2019	MIN	MLB	28	359	149	41.1	.277	-0.7	C(82): 4.7, 1B(1): 0.0	4.4
2020	MIN	MLB	29	455	115	28.4	.279	-0.8	C -8	2.1

Mitch Garver, continued

Batted Ball Distribution

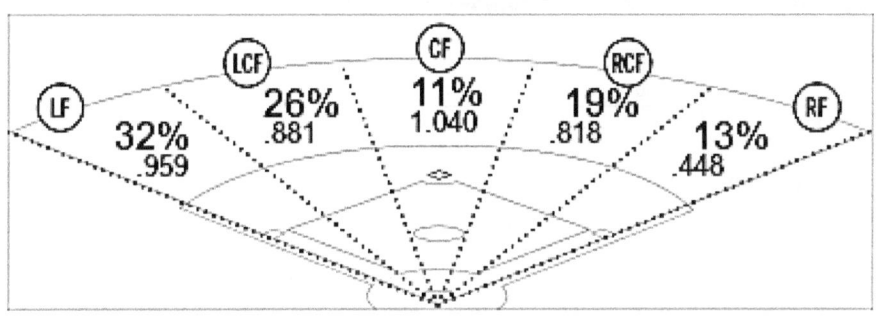

Strike Zone vs LHP Strike Zone vs RHP

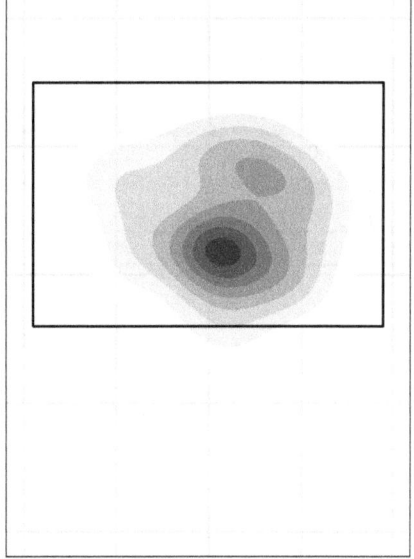

Minnesota Twins 2020

Marwin Gonzalez UT
Born: 03/14/89 Age: 31 Bats: B Throws: R
Height: 6'1" Weight: 205 Origin: International Free Agent, 2005

YEAR	TEAM	LVL	AGE	PA	R	2B	3B	HR	RBI	BB	K	SB	CS	AVG/OBP/SLG
2017	HOU	MLB	28	515	67	34	0	23	90	49	99	8	3	.303/.377/.530
2018	HOU	MLB	29	552	61	25	3	16	68	53	126	2	3	.247/.324/.409
2019	MIN	MLB	30	463	52	19	0	15	55	31	98	1	0	.264/.322/.414
2020	MIN	MLB	31	560	60	28	1	17	65	39	122	8	4	.258/.317/.415

Comparables: Eduardo Escobar, Alex Gonzalez, J.J. Hardy

Once Gonzalez got acclimated following a long free agency, he went on to do what he usually does at the dish. He missed some time with short-term injuries, but by the end of the year he'd cobbled together something approaching league-average offense while logging at least 18 games in each of the four corners. That fits Gonzalez's previous track record and scouting report, and the Twins more or less got what they paid for. One interesting twist worth keeping an eye on this season is how Gonzalez became far more aggressive in the zone in 2019, swinging nearly 68 percent of the time, or well above his career norm (around 60 percent).

YEAR	TEAM	LVL	AGE	PA	DRC+	VORP	BABIP	BRR	FRAA	WARP
2017	HOU	MLB	28	515	124	37.3	.343	-0.8	LF(47): -3.6, SS(38): -1.7	2.5
2018	HOU	MLB	29	552	101	22.4	.301	1.5	LF(73): 0.7, SS(39): -2.7	1.6
2019	MIN	MLB	30	463	92	7.9	.310	-1.2	RF(44): -4.8, 3B(40): 5.0	1.1
2020	MIN	MLB	31	560	93	6.7	.308	-0.3	1B 0, 3B 2	0.8

Marwin Gonzalez, continued

Batted Ball Distribution

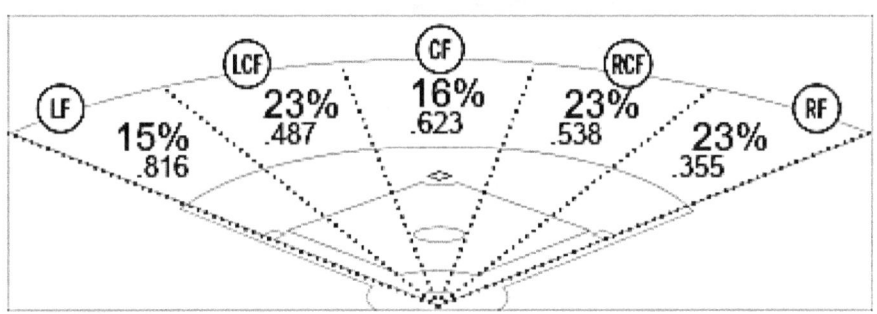

Strike Zone vs LHP   **Strike Zone vs RHP**

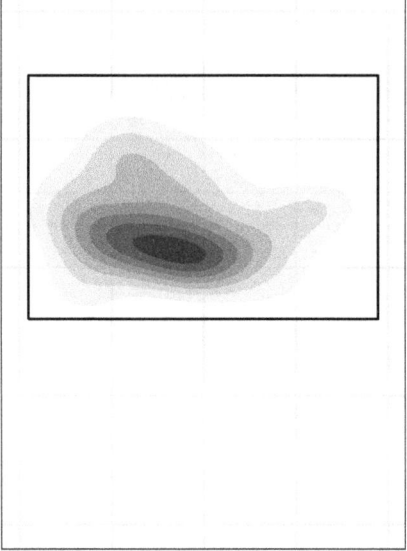

Max Kepler RF

Born: 02/10/93 Age: 27 Bats: L Throws: L
Height: 6'4" Weight: 220 Origin: International Free Agent, 2009

YEAR	TEAM	LVL	AGE	PA	R	2B	3B	HR	RBI	BB	K	SB	CS	AVG/OBP/SLG
2017	MIN	MLB	24	568	67	32	2	19	69	47	114	6	1	.243/.312/.425
2018	MIN	MLB	25	611	80	30	4	20	58	71	96	4	5	.224/.319/.408
2019	MIN	MLB	26	596	98	32	0	36	90	60	99	1	5	.252/.336/.519
2020	MIN	MLB	27	595	75	30	3	28	86	61	104	7	3	.245/.329/.475

Comparables: Mike Marshall, Gregory Polanco, Travis Buck

Making steady, continual progress each year is Kepler's kink. He stayed true to it last season, finding the barrel more often and turning on pitches on the regular. He'll probably never run a high batting average on balls in play, but he makes plenty of contact for his power-hitting ways and has improved against left-handed pitchers. Add in a glove that can play in center, and you've got yourself a quality, prime-aged ballplayer. The five-year extension Kepler signed last off-season already looks like one of the bigger bargains in a sport increasingly defined by bargains.

YEAR	TEAM	LVL	AGE	PA	DRC+	VORP	BABIP	BRR	FRAA	WARP
2017	MIN	MLB	24	568	90	2.0	.276	-2.2	RF(138): 5.1, CF(13): 0.3	0.9
2018	MIN	MLB	25	611	102	16.0	.236	2.7	RF(117): 10.2, CF(55): -1.3	2.9
2019	MIN	MLB	26	596	126	37.4	.244	-3.7	RF(84): 6.0, CF(60): -3.6	3.5
2020	MIN	MLB	27	595	111	23.0	.256	-0.4	RF 6, CF 0	2.9

Max Kepler, continued

Batted Ball Distribution

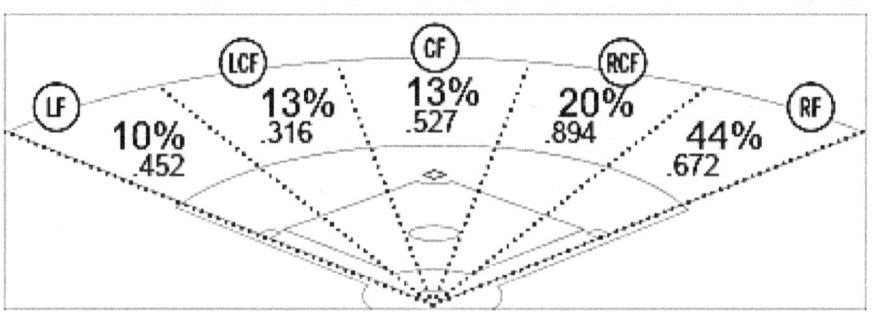

Strike Zone vs LHP   Strike Zone vs RHP

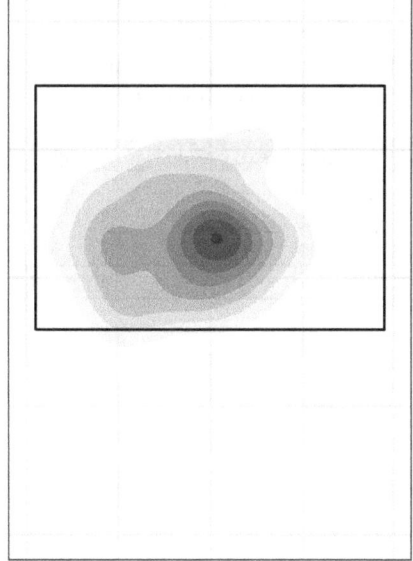

Minnesota Twins 2020

Jorge Polanco   SS
Born: 07/05/93   Age: 26   Bats: B   Throws: R
Height: 5'11"   Weight: 200   Origin: International Free Agent, 2009

YEAR	TEAM	LVL	AGE	PA	R	2B	3B	HR	RBI	BB	K	SB	CS	AVG/OBP/SLG
2017	MIN	MLB	23	544	60	30	3	13	74	41	78	13	5	.256/.313/.410
2018	MIN	MLB	24	333	38	18	3	6	42	25	62	7	7	.288/.345/.427
2019	MIN	MLB	25	704	107	40	7	22	79	60	116	4	3	.295/.356/.485
2020	MIN	MLB	26	595	66	31	4	17	71	47	100	13	6	.273/.334/.440

Comparables: Ketel Marte, Francisco Lindor, Omar Infante

Polanco rewarded the faith the Twins showed when they signed him to a long-term extension during the spring with a strong offensive season. He nearly doubled his barrel rate and scaled way back on slapped contact the other way in favor of driving more balls up the middle and in the air. The adjustments catapulted him into a higher tier of shortstop offense, and better positioning even helped raise his suspect leather into a more passable range. How long he'll be able to stick at shortstop has been a career-dogging question, and it promises to remain a front-and-center concern after offseason ankle surgery. But one thing is for certain: his long, cheap deal will keep him anchored in Minnesota while he answers it.

YEAR	TEAM	LVL	AGE	PA	DRC+	VORP	BABIP	BRR	FRAA	WARP
2017	MIN	MLB	23	544	90	17.7	.278	0.8	SS(130): -9.2	0.9
2018	MIN	MLB	24	333	97	12.6	.345	-3.0	SS(76): -9.7	0.1
2019	MIN	MLB	25	704	119	50.2	.328	4.9	SS(142): -0.7	5.3
2020	MIN	MLB	26	595	104	26.5	.307	0.9	SS -5	2.2

Jorge Polanco, continued

Batted Ball Distribution

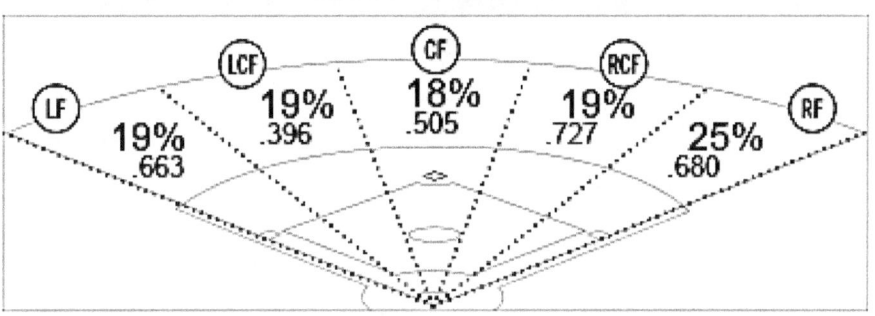

Strike Zone vs LHP **Strike Zone vs RHP**

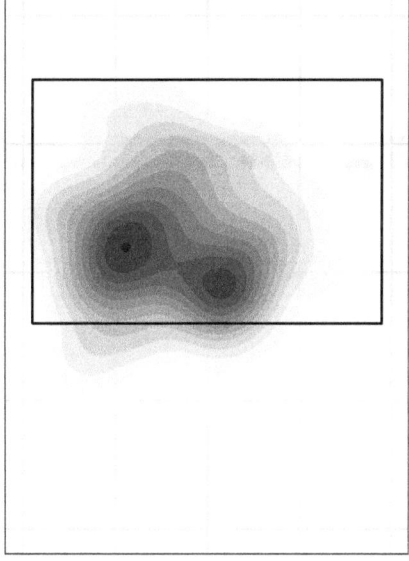

Eddie Rosario   LF

Born: 09/28/91   Age: 28   Bats: L   Throws: R
Height: 6'1"   Weight: 180   Origin: Round 4, 2010 Draft (#135 overall)

YEAR	TEAM	LVL	AGE	PA	R	2B	3B	HR	RBI	BB	K	SB	CS	AVG/OBP/SLG
2017	MIN	MLB	25	589	79	33	2	27	78	35	106	9	8	.290/.328/.507
2018	MIN	MLB	26	592	87	31	2	24	77	30	104	8	2	.288/.323/.479
2019	MIN	MLB	27	590	91	28	1	32	109	22	86	3	1	.276/.300/.500
2020	MIN	MLB	28	560	67	29	3	26	81	25	101	9	4	.273/.306/.485

Comparables: Gerardo Parra, Aaron Rowand, Adam Lind

Whatever questions remained about the staying power of Rosario's offensive production quieted after a third consecutive solidly above-average campaign. You won't find his approach in an instruction manual, as he's among the freest of free-swingers the game has to offer. Yet he makes it work because he's also really good at getting his bat on the ball, as well as yanking it with authority. A midseason ankle injury seemed to stick with Rosario, and his work on both sides of the ball never quite recovered, with his lackluster glovework in particular taking a bite out of his overall value. Rosario will start to get expensive this year, as a solid in-prime player should, but his contact skills should keep him in-demand.

YEAR	TEAM	LVL	AGE	PA	DRC+	VORP	BABIP	BRR	FRAA	WARP
2017	MIN	MLB	25	589	107	18.9	.312	-1.6	LF(138): -2.7, RF(16): 0.2	1.6
2018	MIN	MLB	26	592	112	29.4	.316	6.8	LF(125): 5.9, RF(5): -0.2	3.6
2019	MIN	MLB	27	590	109	23.2	.273	0.9	LF(124): -8.8, RF(11): -0.5	1.5
2020	MIN	MLB	28	560	104	19.6	.293	1.7	LF -5, RF 0	1.5

Eddie Rosario, continued

Batted Ball Distribution

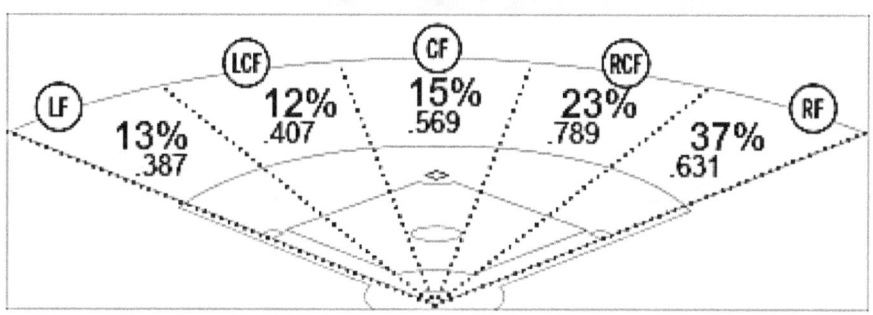

Strike Zone vs LHP   **Strike Zone vs RHP**

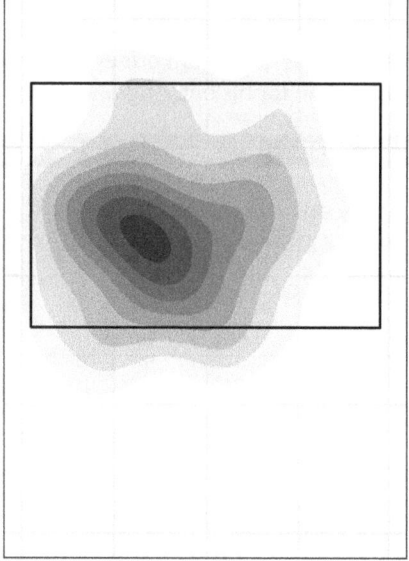

Miguel Sanó 3B
Born: 05/11/93   Age: 27   Bats: R   Throws: R
Height: 6'4"   Weight: 272   Origin: International Free Agent, 2009

YEAR	TEAM	LVL	AGE	PA	R	2B	3B	HR	RBI	BB	K	SB	CS	AVG/OBP/SLG
2017	MIN	MLB	24	483	75	15	2	28	77	54	173	0	0	.264/.352/.507
2018	FTM	A+	25	77	11	2	0	2	12	13	21	0	0	.328/.442/.453
2018	ROC	AAA	25	36	2	1	0	2	5	6	8	0	0	.267/.389/.500
2018	MIN	MLB	25	299	32	14	0	13	41	31	115	0	0	.199/.281/.398
2019	MIN	MLB	26	439	76	19	2	34	79	55	159	0	1	.247/.346/.576
2020	MIN	MLB	27	560	82	26	1	38	98	67	201	1	1	.247/.341/.540

Comparables: Gary Sánchez, Brandon Allen, Randal Grichuk

In a make-or-break year, Sanó finally, mercifully made. An offseason heel injury delayed his seasonal debut, and a brutal six-week stretch as the weather warmed threatened his opportunity. But a two-homer outburst at the end of June begot a second-half onslaught the likes of which Twins fans have pined for. He broke out over the season's final three months, racking up elite exit velocities, dingers and signature moments. Our defensive metrics continued to like him a lot more than our eyes, but let's be clear: the Twins continue to employ him for his bat. And his bat seems on the upswing.

YEAR	TEAM	LVL	AGE	PA	DRC+	VORP	BABIP	BRR	FRAA	WARP
2017	MIN	MLB	24	483	119	23.1	.375	-2.0	3B(82): -5.9, 1B(9): 1.2	1.9
2018	FTM	A+	25	77	169	7.8	.463	0.2	3B(10): 0.4	0.8
2018	ROC	AAA	25	36	130	2.7	.300	0.2	3B(4): 1.5, 1B(1): 0.0	0.4
2018	MIN	MLB	25	299	83	-0.5	.286	-1.0	3B(56): 0.1, 1B(11): 0.1	0.2
2019	MIN	MLB	26	439	128	31.7	.319	-2.5	3B(91): -3.2, 1B(9): -0.6	2.5
2020	MIN	MLB	27	560	130	32.5	.331	-1.9	3B -2, 1B 1	3.3

Miguel Sanó, continued

Batted Ball Distribution

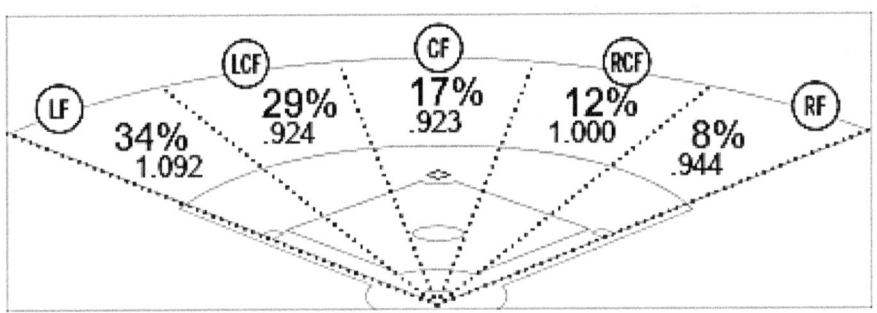

Strike Zone vs LHP   **Strike Zone vs RHP**

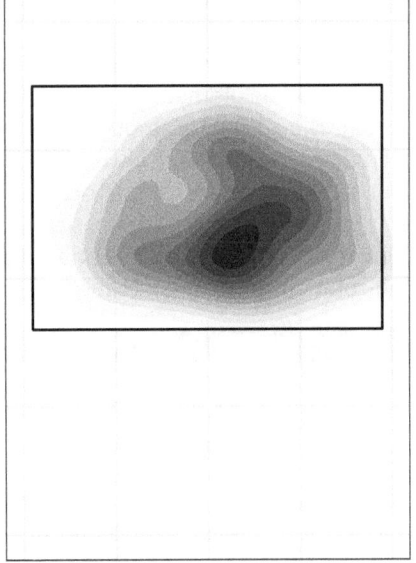

Minnesota Twins 2020

Homer Bailey RHP
Born: 05/03/86   Age: 34   Bats: R   Throws: R
Height: 6'4"   Weight: 223   Origin: Round 1, 2004 Draft (#7 overall)

YEAR	TEAM	LVL	AGE	W	L	SV	G	GS	IP	H	HR	BB/9	K/9	K	GB%	BABIP
2017	DYT	A	31	1	0	0	1	1	6	1	0	0.0	9.0	6	54%	.077
2017	CIN	MLB	31	6	9	0	18	18	91	112	11	4.2	6.6	67	46%	.346
2018	LOU	AAA	32	2	2	0	7	6	37^2	41	4	2.4	6.7	28	37%	.311
2018	CIN	MLB	32	1	14	0	20	20	106^1	141	23	2.8	6.3	75	44%	.327
2019	OAK	MLB	33	6	3	0	13	13	73^1	73	9	1.8	8.3	68	44%	.300
2019	KCA	MLB	33	7	6	0	18	18	90	89	12	3.8	8.1	81	46%	.301
2020	MIN	MLB	34	9	7	0	24	24	129	137	19	3.1	8.1	116	44%	.312

Comparables: Ervin Santana, Matt Garza, Edwin Jackson

After watching Bailey implode yet again last April, it was easy to think "Does anyone get less out of good stuff than this guy?" When the A's acquired the always-talented, usually-lousy righty last July, the move had more than a whiff of "we're out of functional bodies" desperation to it. All of which is to say that Bailey's 13 starts with Oakland went better than anyone could have possibly expected. He halved his walk rate from recent years while limiting damage on contact, and he ultimately produced 1.6 very crucial WARP for the A's down the stretch. The abrupt turnaround stemmed from the kind of adjustments everyone else is making: fewer sinkers, more of his best secondary (an excellent split, in this case), and better location on his fastballs. It seems simple, but he isn't the first guy to post dramatically better results after a few modest changes. Provided that he returns to his new well, there's no reason to think he can't be a mid-rotation starter again. Nine lives, this cat.

YEAR	TEAM	LVL	AGE	WHIP	ERA	DRA	WARP	MPH	FB%	WHF	CSP
2017	DYT	A	31	0.17	0.00	2.38	0.2				
2017	CIN	MLB	31	1.69	6.43	7.38	-1.8	95.7	57	10.2	48
2018	LOU	AAA	32	1.35	4.78	5.70	-0.1				
2018	CIN	MLB	32	1.64	6.09	6.03	-0.9	95.7	56	9.8	49.6
2019	OAK	MLB	33	1.20	4.30	3.72	1.6	95.2	52.5	12.2	50.2
2019	KCA	MLB	33	1.41	4.80	5.42	0.3	95.6	49.1	11.2	47
2020	MIN	MLB	34	1.40	4.86	4.77	1.2	94.4	52.5	10.7	48

Homer Bailey, continued

Pitch Shape vs LHH

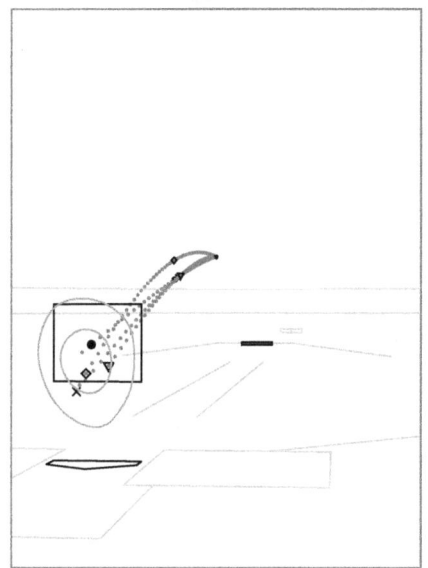

Pitch Shape vs RHH

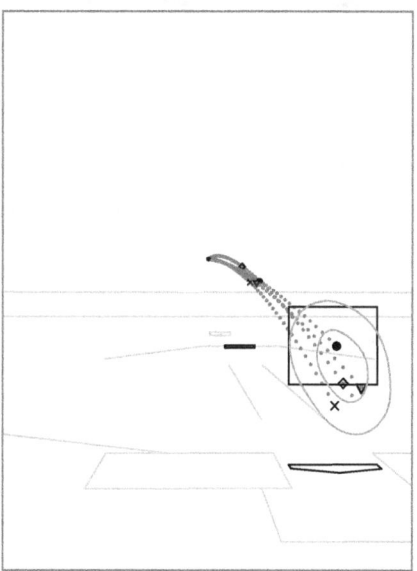

Type	Frequency	Velocity	H Movement	V Movement
● Fastball	49.5%	93.4 [103]	-6.8 [100]	-14.6 [104]
☐ Sinker				
+ Cutter				
▲ Changeup				
✕ Splitter	25.6%	84.5 [98]	-6.2 [106]	-30.9 [94]
▽ Slider	15.0%	87.7 [114]	2.4 [89]	-26.6 [119]
◇ Curveball	8.9%	78.8 [101]	9.4 [108]	-47.1 [101]
⊕ Slow Curveball				
✱ Knuckleball				
▼ Screwball				

José Berríos RHP

Born: 05/27/94   Age: 26   Bats: R   Throws: R
Height: 6'0"   Weight: 205   Origin: Round 1, 2012 Draft (#32 overall)

YEAR	TEAM	LVL	AGE	W	L	SV	G	GS	IP	H	HR	BB/9	K/9	K	GB%	BABIP
2017	ROC	AAA	23	3	0	0	6	6	39^2	24	2	1.8	8.8	39	40%	.214
2017	MIN	MLB	23	14	8	0	26	25	145^2	131	15	3.0	8.6	139	41%	.289
2018	MIN	MLB	24	12	11	0	32	32	192^1	159	25	2.9	9.5	202	43%	.270
2019	MIN	MLB	25	14	8	0	32	32	200^1	194	26	2.3	8.8	195	43%	.299
2020	MIN	MLB	26	13	9	0	29	29	184	179	28	2.9	9.0	184	42%	.301

Comparables: Archie Bradley, Lucas Giolito, Eduardo Rodriguez

Berríos' signature curveball swept more than ever last season, but he paid for the longer movement trajectory with a reduced whiff rate. He left more of 'em hanging than usual, too. Berríos was able to offset his bendy losses with faded gains, however, as he dramatically improved his changeup performance. In the end, he left some whiffs on the table, but the eventual result was everything on the top lines remaining eerily in agreement with his prior seasons. Though he's not quite an ace (yet), he'll be 25 until the end of May, and it still feels like there's a next gear here. With his arbitration years hurtling closer, the Twins will hope that he finds it on the sooner side of later.

YEAR	TEAM	LVL	AGE	WHIP	ERA	DRA	WARP	MPH	FB%	WHF	CSP
2017	ROC	AAA	23	0.81	1.13	1.84	1.7				
2017	MIN	MLB	23	1.23	3.89	4.29	2.1	96.0	61.5	10.5	46.4
2018	MIN	MLB	24	1.14	3.84	4.25	2.4	95.5	60.4	12.3	46.7
2019	MIN	MLB	25	1.22	3.68	4.44	2.9	95.2	55.2	11.4	48.4
2020	MIN	MLB	26	1.30	4.37	4.39	2.4	95.1	59.4	11.8	48.2

José Berríos, continued

Pitch Shape vs LHH

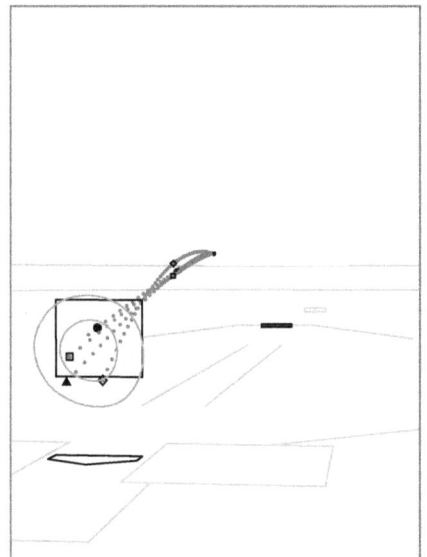

Pitch Shape vs RHH

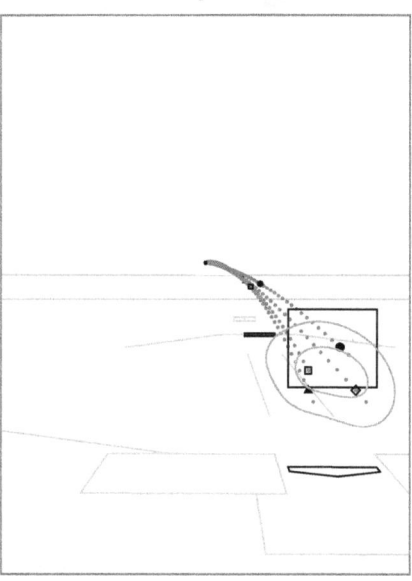

Type	Frequency	Velocity	H Movement	V Movement
● Fastball	32.2%	93.5 [103]	-8.5 [93]	-15 [102]
☐ Sinker	23.1%	92.5 [99]	-14.1 [90]	-20.4 [100]
+ Cutter				
▲ Changeup	15.9%	82.9 [91]	-12.6 [93]	-32.9 [84]
✕ Splitter				
▽ Slider				
◇ Curveball	28.9%	81.6 [110]	15.2 [131]	-39.5 [117]
✦ Slow Curveball				
✱ Knuckleball				
▼ Screwball				

Minnesota Twins 2020

Jhoulys Chacín RHP

Born: 01/07/88 Age: 32 Bats: R Throws: R
Height: 6'3" Weight: 215 Origin: International Free Agent, 2004

YEAR	TEAM	LVL	AGE	W	L	SV	G	GS	IP	H	HR	BB/9	K/9	K	GB%	BABIP
2017	SDN	MLB	29	13	10	0	32	32	180^1	157	19	3.6	7.6	153	50%	.272
2018	MIL	MLB	30	15	8	0	35	35	192^2	153	18	3.3	7.3	156	44%	.250
2019	BOS	MLB	31	0	2	0	6	5	14^2	16	6	4.3	12.9	21	38%	.303
2019	MIL	MLB	31	3	10	0	19	19	88^2	99	19	4.0	8.1	80	38%	.308
2020	BOS	MLB	32	2	2	0	33	0	35	34	6	3.6	7.8	30	41%	.287

Comparables: Clay Buchholz, Trevor Cahill, Aaron Sele

One season after serving as the de facto ace of an exciting Brewers team, Chacín performed so poorly that he earned a DFA in late August. Sometimes it can be difficult to pinpoint exactly why pitchers see their performance fluctuate so wildly, but in the case of Chacín, it's pretty simple: too many damn homers. His home-run rate nearly *tripled*, and while Rob Manfred would probably look at that stat and give you his best Bernard Lowe—"this doesn't look like anything to me"—it's fairly obvious what's to blame. Chacín didn't lose velocity. He didn't substantially alter his pitch mix. He wasn't hurt. We're just to believe that he turned into a JUGS machine overnight. If MLB ever does come clean about whatever baseball shenanigans occurred in 2019, Chacín should file a grievance. Considering he ended the year as a Red Sox starter, perhaps he should sue for emotional damages, too.

YEAR	TEAM	LVL	AGE	WHIP	ERA	DRA	WARP	MPH	FB%	WHF	CSP
2017	SDN	MLB	29	1.27	3.89	4.50	2.2	93.7	54.1	8.6	48.2
2018	MIL	MLB	30	1.16	3.50	4.51	1.8	92.5	48.1	9.1	48.9
2019	BOS	MLB	31	1.57	7.36	3.83	0.3	91.7	44.3	10	46.5
2019	MIL	MLB	31	1.56	5.79	6.96	-1.2	92.1	44.3	8.6	47.4
2020	BOS	MLB	32	1.38	4.55	4.68	0.2	91.8	48.2	8.8	47.6

Jhoulys Chacín, continued

Pitch Shape vs LHH

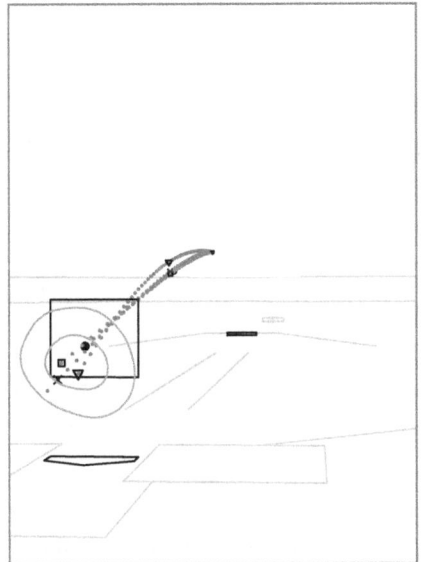

Pitch Shape vs RHH

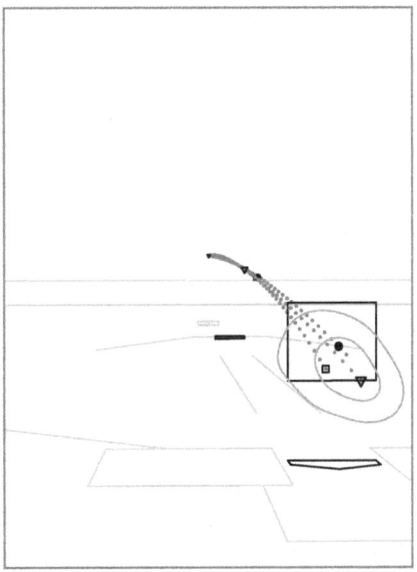

Type	Frequency	Velocity	H Movement	V Movement
● Fastball	13.0%	90.4 [94]	-6.1 [103]	-17.3 [96]
□ Sinker	30.6%	90.2 [88]	-13.2 [96]	-23 [91]
+ Cutter				
▲ Changeup				
✕ Splitter	5.6%	83.2 [92]	-7.7 [101]	-30.2 [96]
▽ Slider	49.4%	80.1 [82]	11.6 [127]	-34.9 [95]
◇ Curveball				
⊕ Slow Curveball				
✹ Knuckleball				
▼ Screwball				

Tyler Clippard   RHP
Born: 02/14/85   Age: 35   Bats: R   Throws: R
Height: 6'3"   Weight: 200   Origin: Round 9, 2003 Draft (#274 overall)

YEAR	TEAM	LVL	AGE	W	L	SV	G	GS	IP	H	HR	BB/9	K/9	K	GB%	BABIP
2017	NYA	MLB	32	1	5	1	40	0	36^1	28	7	4.7	10.4	42	35%	.236
2017	CHA	MLB	32	1	1	2	11	0	10	8	0	4.5	10.8	12	30%	.296
2017	HOU	MLB	32	0	2	2	16	0	14	11	3	4.5	11.6	18	36%	.242
2018	TOR	MLB	33	4	3	7	73	1	68^2	57	13	3.0	11.1	85	22%	.272
2019	CLE	MLB	34	1	0	0	53	3	62	38	8	2.2	9.3	64	33%	.204
2020	MIN	MLB	35	2	2	0	44	0	46	37	9	3.2	10.1	52	30%	.248

Comparables: Eric Gagne, Rafael Soriano, Juan Cruz

Did you know: Clippard added a ninth jersey to his collection in 2019 by pitching for Cleveland? In doing so, he passed Rich Hill for the third-most teams played for by an active player. More importantly, did you know: Clippard pitched *well*? He still gave up his share of home runs, but not as many as you'd suspect given the altered baseball and his history of gopheritis—heck, it's enough to make one wonder if the lobster, with its institutional knowledge of being boiled, might be the being best suited to survive climate change. Clippard is now 35 and the Twins will be his tenth major-league employer, but he'll need to try to extend his career much further if he wants to give Edwin Jackson a run for his wardrobe.

YEAR	TEAM	LVL	AGE	WHIP	ERA	DRA	WARP	MPH	FB%	WHF	CSP
2017	NYA	MLB	32	1.29	4.95	2.86	0.9	92.6	40.4	15.9	43.9
2017	CHA	MLB	32	1.30	1.80	2.76	0.3	93.2	32.9	14.5	41.2
2017	HOU	MLB	32	1.29	6.43	3.48	0.3	92.3	36.3	12.6	47.3
2018	TOR	MLB	33	1.17	3.67	3.55	1.1	92.9	41.8	15.8	45.5
2019	CLE	MLB	34	0.85	2.90	4.14	0.8	91.4	40.8	14.2	46.1
2020	MIN	MLB	35	1.15	3.79	3.94	0.6	91.0	39.7	14.7	44.6

Tyler Clippard, continued

Pitch Shape vs LHH

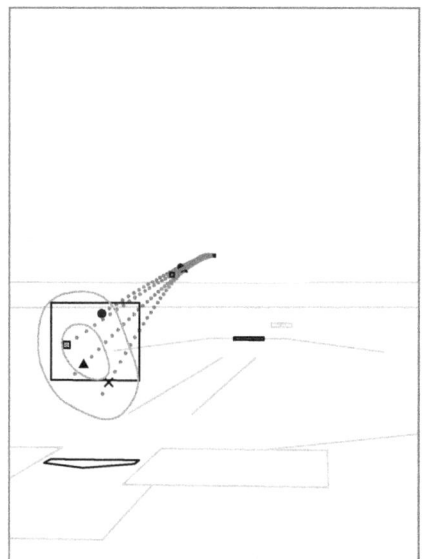

Pitch Shape vs RHH

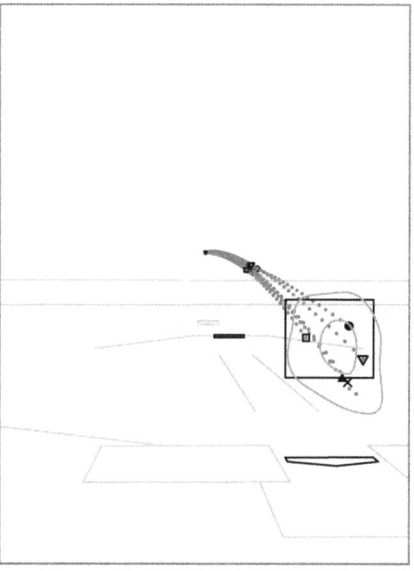

Type	Frequency	Velocity	H Movement	V Movement
● Fastball	21.4%	90.4 [94]	-5.5 [106]	-12.6 [109]
□ Sinker	19.4%	90 [87]	-11.2 [109]	-17.1 [112]
+ Cutter				
▲ Changeup	30.5%	78.7 [76]	-10.8 [102]	-25.7 [105]
✕ Splitter	19.5%	82 [86]	-1.8 [123]	-38.1 [70]
▽ Slider	5.4%	83.5 [96]	3.3 [93]	-31.2 [105]
◇ Curveball	3.9%	74.5 [86]	5.8 [93]	-55.8 [83]
⊕ Slow Curveball				
✱ Knuckleball				
▼ Screwball				

Randy Dobnak RHP

Born: 01/17/95   Age: 25   Bats: R   Throws: R
Height: 6'1"   Weight: 230   Origin: Undrafted Free Agent, 2017

YEAR	TEAM	LVL	AGE	W	L	SV	G	GS	IP	H	HR	BB/9	K/9	K	GB%	BABIP
2017	ELZ	RK	22	2	0	1	5	3	26¹	19	3	2.1	7.5	22	46%	.225
2017	CDR	A	22	0	0	0	1	1	7	6	0	1.3	1.3	1	56%	.240
2018	CDR	A	23	10	5	0	24	20	129	138	6	1.7	5.9	84	47%	.314
2019	FTM	A+	24	3	0	0	4	4	22¹	18	0	1.6	5.6	14	59%	.273
2019	PEN	AA	24	4	2	0	11	10	66²	58	6	0.8	8.2	61	60%	.278
2019	ROC	AAA	24	5	2	0	9	7	46	28	0	3.5	6.7	34	62%	.229
2019	MIN	MLB	24	2	1	1	9	5	28¹	27	1	1.6	7.3	23	54%	.302
2020	MIN	MLB	25	4	3	0	21	10	63	61	7	3.1	8.3	58	56%	.299

Comparables: Taylor Jordan, Brock Stewart, Phil Irwin

You want a story for the silver screen? How about Dobnak's: undrafted D-II pitcher, independent league hustler, Uber driver, bespectacled horseshoe mustache wearer and now accomplished big-league starter. He began his year in High-A and ended it as Minnesota's Game 2 starter—an assignment that, when combined with his former side gig, casted simultaneous spotlights on both the obscenity of non-living wages paid to up-and-coming ballplayers and the insufferability of Yankees fans, who razzed him with "U-ber!" chants. Sinker-slider combinations aren't exactly en vogue right now, but Dobnak's is a solid one, and his results to date suggest a deserved spot in the rotation or (at least) in the bullpen to begin 2020.

YEAR	TEAM	LVL	AGE	WHIP	ERA	DRA	WARP	MPH	FB%	WHF	CSP
2017	ELZ	RK	22	0.95	2.39	1.91	1.1				
2017	CDR	A	22	1.00	2.57	4.57	0.1				
2018	CDR	A	23	1.26	3.14	4.44	1.1				
2019	FTM	A+	24	0.99	0.40	3.78	0.3				
2019	PEN	AA	24	0.96	2.57	3.67	1.0				
2019	ROC	AAA	24	1.00	2.15	2.47	1.8				
2019	MIN	MLB	24	1.13	1.59	4.60	0.3	94.5	59	14	46.4
2020	MIN	MLB	25	1.31	4.08	4.08	1.0	94.2	60.4	14.4	47.5

Randy Dobnak, continued

Pitch Shape vs LHH

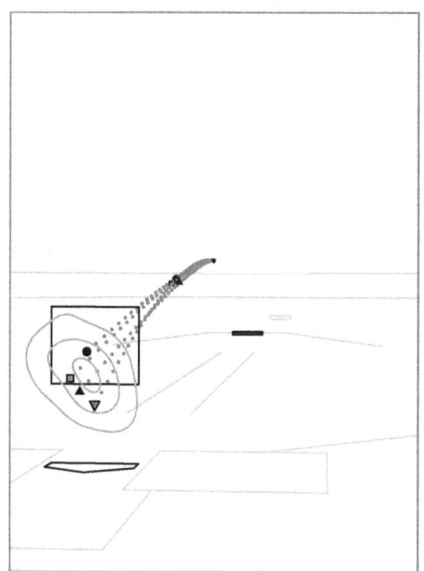

Pitch Shape vs RHH

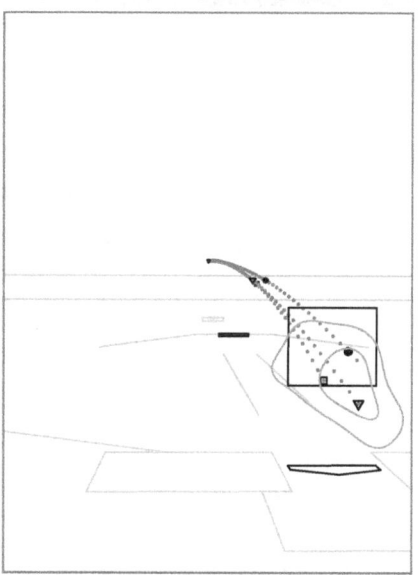

Type	Frequency	Velocity	H Movement	V Movement
● Fastball	23.0%	93.3 [102]	-9.2 [90]	-20.6 [88]
☐ Sinker	36.1%	92.1 [97]	-12.3 [102]	-27.8 [74]
+ Cutter				
▲ Changeup	13.1%	85.7 [101]	-13.2 [90]	-29.8 [93]
✕ Splitter				
▽ Slider	27.9%	84 [98]	2.5 [90]	-37.2 [88]
◇ Curveball				
⊕ Slow Curveball				
✱ Knuckleball				
▼ Screwball				

Tyler Duffey RHP

Born: 12/27/90 Age: 29 Bats: R Throws: R
Height: 6'3" Weight: 220 Origin: Round 5, 2012 Draft (#160 overall)

YEAR	TEAM	LVL	AGE	W	L	SV	G	GS	IP	H	HR	BB/9	K/9	K	GB%	BABIP
2017	MIN	MLB	26	2	3	1	56	0	71	79	9	2.3	8.5	67	50%	.326
2018	ROC	AAA	27	4	4	3	31	0	59	48	5	3.1	9.6	63	45%	.277
2018	MIN	MLB	27	2	2	0	19	1	25	26	6	1.4	6.8	19	35%	.260
2019	ROC	AAA	28	0	0	1	7	0	13^2	8	0	3.3	14.5	22	48%	.320
2019	MIN	MLB	28	5	1	0	58	0	57^2	44	8	2.2	12.8	82	38%	.275
2020	MIN	MLB	29	3	3	0	60	0	64	58	9	2.6	10.7	76	40%	.307

Comparables: Zach McAllister, Jerad Eickhoff, Trevor Oaks

Minnesota's emphasis on pitch development paid huge dividends for Duffey, who transformed his breaking ball in-season—from a downer with too much hump into a hard, tight hook that devastated hitters in the second half. Long an electric arm without the consistency to stick in the rotation, or quite enough raw stuff to dominate in the pen, Duffey finally got the recipe right in 2019—and boy, did it result in a ton of empty swings. Provided his gains stick, he'll represent an analytic victory for the new regime—and a mighty fine late-inning reliever to boot.

YEAR	TEAM	LVL	AGE	WHIP	ERA	DRA	WARP	MPH	FB%	WHF	CSP
2017	MIN	MLB	26	1.37	4.94	3.65	1.2	94.0	59.4	11.8	48
2018	ROC	AAA	27	1.15	2.90	3.35	1.2				
2018	MIN	MLB	27	1.20	7.20	5.41	-0.1	95.4	61.2	11.3	48.5
2019	ROC	AAA	28	0.95	1.32	2.36	0.5				
2019	MIN	MLB	28	1.01	2.50	3.05	1.4	96.1	54	16.7	47
2020	MIN	MLB	29	1.20	3.75	3.80	1.0	94.6	57	14.1	47.8

Tyler Duffey, continued

Pitch Shape vs LHH

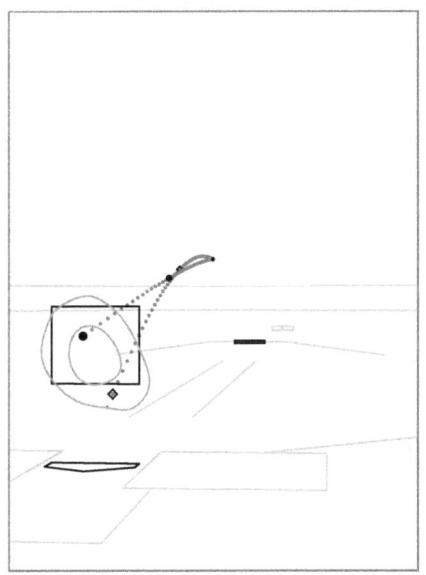

Pitch Shape vs RHH

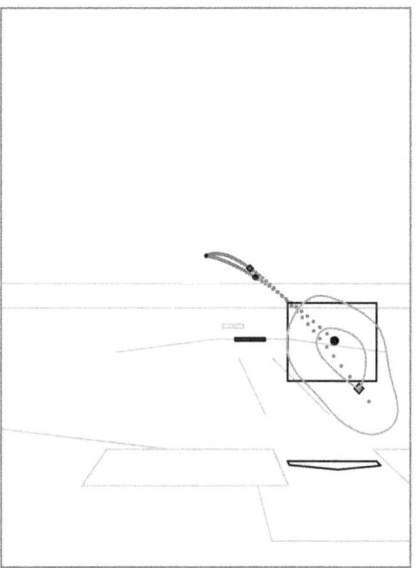

Type	Frequency	Velocity	H Movement	V Movement
● Fastball	51.5%	94.3 [105]	-5 [108]	-13.8 [105]
☐ Sinker				
+ Cutter				
▲ Changeup				
✕ Splitter				
▽ Slider				
◇ Curveball	45.5%	82.5 [113]	5.3 [91]	-46.4 [103]
⊕ Slow Curveball				
✳ Knuckleball				
▼ Screwball				

Sam Dyson RHP
Born: 05/07/88 Age: 32 Bats: R Throws: R
Height: 6'1" Weight: 212 Origin: Round 4, 2010 Draft (#126 overall)

YEAR	TEAM	LVL	AGE	W	L	SV	G	GS	IP	H	HR	BB/9	K/9	K	GB%	BABIP
2017	TEX	MLB	29	1	6	0	17	0	16^2	31	6	6.5	3.8	7	62%	.379
2017	SFN	MLB	29	3	4	14	38	0	38	36	2	4.3	6.4	27	67%	.286
2018	SFN	MLB	30	4	3	3	74	0	70^1	56	5	2.6	7.2	56	62%	.270
2019	MIN	MLB	31	1	0	0	12	0	11^1	14	3	4.8	6.4	8	51%	.306
2019	SFN	MLB	31	4	1	2	49	0	51	39	3	1.2	8.3	47	58%	.265
2020	MIN	MLB	32	2	2	0	33	0	35	35	5	3.0	8.1	32	58%	.302

Comparables: Jeremy Jeffress, Brandon League, Blake Treinen

In November, MLB opened an investigation into two Instagram posts by Dyson's ex-girlfriend alleging physical and emotional abuse against her and acts of animal cruelty against the couple's cat. As of press time this investigation remains open.

YEAR	TEAM	LVL	AGE	WHIP	ERA	DRA	WARP	MPH	FB%	WHF	CSP
2017	TEX	MLB	29	2.58	10.80	8.89	-0.7	96.9	73.8	6	47.2
2017	SFN	MLB	29	1.42	4.03	6.27	-0.5	96.9	73.8	10	48.3
2018	SFN	MLB	30	1.08	2.69	4.01	0.7	96.0	65.4	11.9	48.8
2019	MIN	MLB	31	1.76	7.15	6.37	-0.1	95.0	57.8	7	51.5
2019	SFN	MLB	31	0.90	2.47	3.18	1.2	95.6	57.8	9.6	49
2020	MIN	MLB	32	1.33	4.37	4.35	0.3	95.0	64	9.8	48.5

Sam Dyson, *continued*

Pitch Shape vs LHH

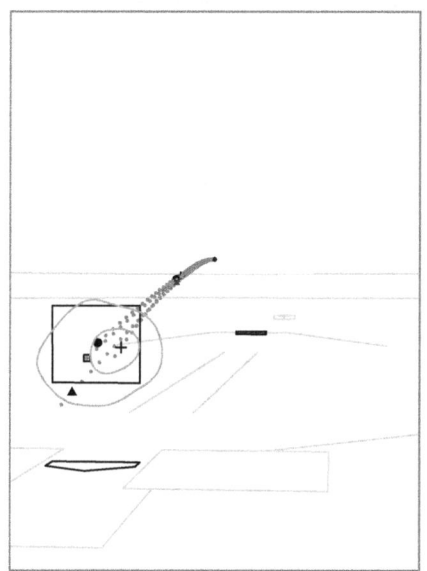

Pitch Shape vs RHH

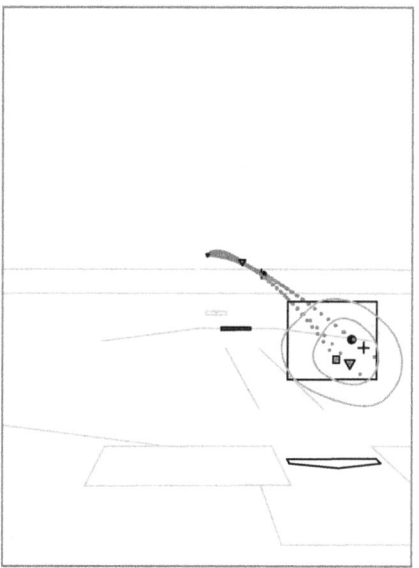

Type	Frequency	Velocity	H Movement	V Movement
● Fastball	13.0%	94 [105]	-6.3 [102]	-17.6 [96]
☐ Sinker	45.5%	94 [107]	-14.4 [89]	-24.9 [84]
+ Cutter	23.8%	91 [115]	1.5 [98]	-22.7 [105]
▲ Changeup	10.3%	87.5 [108]	-14.2 [86]	-31 [89]
✕ Splitter				
▽ Slider	7.4%	83.3 [96]	14.5 [140]	-42.9 [72]
◇ Curveball				
✦ Slow Curveball				
✶ Knuckleball				
▼ Screwball				

Cory Gearrin RHP

Born: 04/14/86   Age: 34   Bats: R   Throws: R
Height: 6'1"   Weight: 205   Origin: Round 4, 2007 Draft (#138 overall)

YEAR	TEAM	LVL	AGE	W	L	SV	G	GS	IP	H	HR	BB/9	K/9	K	GB%	BABIP
2017	SFN	MLB	31	4	3	0	68	0	68	50	4	4.6	8.5	64	49%	.263
2018	SFN	MLB	32	1	1	1	35	0	30	33	5	3.9	9.3	31	34%	.329
2018	TEX	MLB	32	1	0	0	21	0	21¹	13	2	2.5	8.4	20	52%	.212
2018	OAK	MLB	32	0	0	0	6	0	6	10	0	3.0	3.0	2	50%	.417
2019	SEA	MLB	33	0	2	0	48	2	41¹	38	3	4.6	8.5	39	47%	.310
2019	NYA	MLB	33	1	1	0	18	0	14	17	2	2.6	5.1	8	43%	.319
2020	NYA	MLB	34	2	2	0	33	0	35	35	5	3.8	8.5	33	45%	.302

Comparables: Ricky Bottalico, Al Reyes, David Aardsma

Imagine the "guy tapping his temple" meme for a second. Good. Now picture Gearrin. If you're always balking, you can never be charged with a balk. The most interesting aspect of his season was the weird toe tap he does before every pitch, which at one point was okay, then it was illegal, then it was allowed again. Riveting stuff. It's not just movement on the rubber that has people's heads spinning though—Gearrin has now made his way through five teams in the last two seasons.

YEAR	TEAM	LVL	AGE	WHIP	ERA	DRA	WARP	MPH	FB%	WHF	CSP
2017	SFN	MLB	31	1.25	1.99	5.60	-0.3	94.0	54.7	12.5	48.6
2018	SFN	MLB	32	1.53	4.20	4.57	0.1	94.3	48.9	12.2	44.3
2018	TEX	MLB	32	0.89	2.53	4.97	0.0	93.6	49	12.4	46.6
2018	OAK	MLB	32	2.00	6.00	3.91	0.1	93.7	60	7.6	51.4
2019	SEA	MLB	33	1.43	3.92	4.95	0.2	93.4	46.1	10.3	46
2019	NYA	MLB	33	1.50	4.50	6.84	-0.2	93.5	40	5	52.2
2020	NYA	MLB	34	1.41	4.67	4.70	0.2	92.6	48.5	10.7	46.6

Cory Gearrin, continued

Pitch Shape vs LHH

Pitch Shape vs RHH

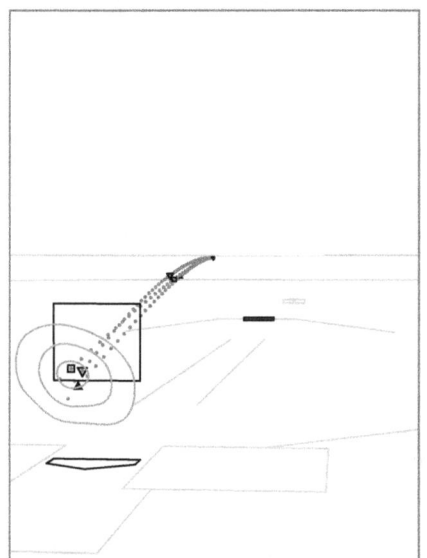
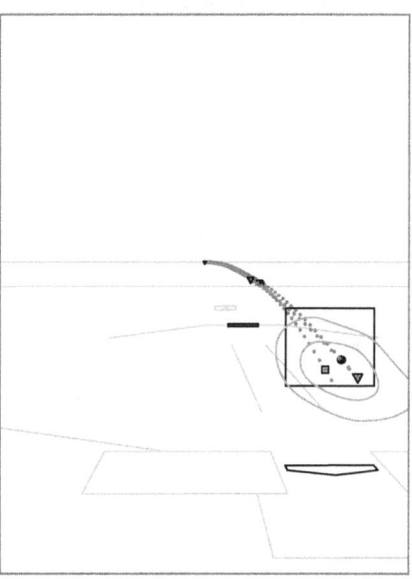

Type	Frequency	Velocity	H Movement	V Movement
● Fastball	5.7%	91.4 [97]	-13.6 [70]	-21.8 [85]
☐ Sinker	38.8%	91.6 [95]	-16.9 [72]	-27.4 [75]
+ Cutter				
▲ Changeup	15.1%	85.6 [101]	-15.1 [81]	-34.5 [79]
✕ Splitter				
▽ Slider	40.5%	85.6 [105]	3.5 [94]	-29.4 [111]
◇ Curveball				
⊕ Slow Curveball				
✳ Knuckleball				
▼ Screwball				

Blaine Hardy LHP

Born: 03/14/87 Age: 33 Bats: L Throws: L
Height: 6'2" Weight: 218 Origin: Round 22, 2008 Draft (#655 overall)

YEAR	TEAM	LVL	AGE	W	L	SV	G	GS	IP	H	HR	BB/9	K/9	K	GB%	BABIP
2017	TOL	AAA	30	7	3	3	34	2	40²	32	1	1.1	10.0	45	48%	.304
2017	DET	MLB	30	1	0	0	35	0	33¹	46	7	3.5	7.6	28	34%	.361
2018	TOL	AAA	31	3	0	0	9	4	26¹	14	0	1.4	11.6	34	39%	.250
2018	DET	MLB	31	4	5	1	30	13	86	79	10	2.3	6.9	66	42%	.275
2019	DET	MLB	32	1	1	0	39	0	44¹	38	10	2.6	5.9	29	50%	.215
2020	MIN	MLB	33	2	2	0	33	0	35	35	7	2.8	6.6	26	46%	.275

Comparables: Dan Jennings, Sam Freeman, Luis García

Hardy is the inverse of a Clint Eastwood baseball movie: He has trouble with everything but the curve. The lefty was wrecked by, of all demographics, his own kind last year (seven HR in 59 plate appearances) before being medically wrecked by a flexor tendon strain. The curve remains his golden calf, and he began setting up more with a changeup rather than his upper-80s fastball. Hardy's experience overwhelming you with soft stuff should help him transition to a post-baseball career as a MyPillow spokesperson.

YEAR	TEAM	LVL	AGE	WHIP	ERA	DRA	WARP	MPH	FB%	WHF	CSP
2017	TOL	AAA	30	0.91	3.10	2.35	1.3				
2017	DET	MLB	30	1.77	5.94	5.24	0.0	91.7	44.9	11.3	49.8
2018	TOL	AAA	31	0.68	1.03	2.40	0.9				
2018	DET	MLB	31	1.17	3.56	3.98	1.2	90.2	32.9	9.1	51.5
2019	DET	MLB	32	1.15	4.47	4.75	0.3	90.4	22.5	10.5	47.8
2020	MIN	MLB	33	1.32	4.59	4.78	0.2	89.5	31.2	9.8	48.9

Blaine Hardy, continued

Pitch Shape vs LHH

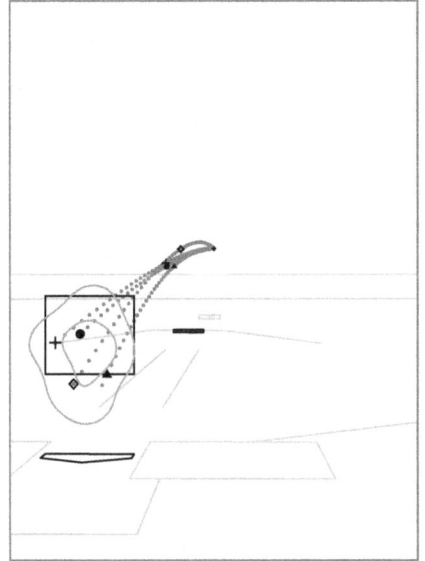

Pitch Shape vs RHH

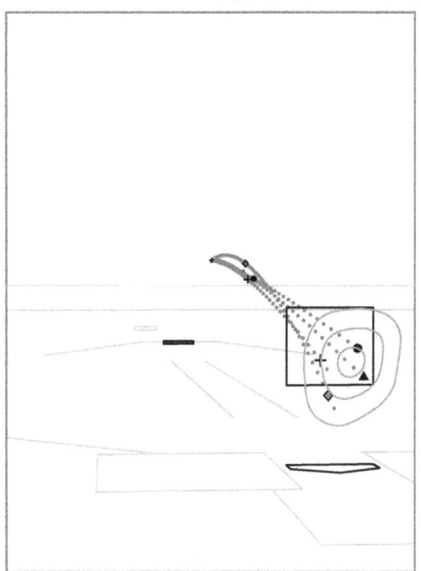

Type	Frequency	Velocity	H Movement	V Movement
● Fastball	21.3%	88.7 [89]	7.1 [99]	-14.8 [103]
□ Sinker				
+ Cutter	12.6%	86.4 [86]	-1.8 [100]	-21.8 [109]
▲ Changeup	44.8%	79.6 [79]	15.2 [81]	-30.2 [92]
✕ Splitter				
▽ Slider				
◇ Curveball	20.0%	76.8 [94]	-5.1 [90]	-55 [84]
⊕ Slow Curveball				
✱ Knuckleball				
▼ Screwball				

Rich Hill LHP

Born: 03/11/80   Age: 40   Bats: L   Throws: L
Height: 6'5"   Weight: 221   Origin: Round 4, 2002 Draft (#112 overall)

YEAR	TEAM	LVL	AGE	W	L	SV	G	GS	IP	H	HR	BB/9	K/9	K	GB%	BABIP
2017	LAN	MLB	37	12	8	0	25	25	135^2	99	18	3.3	11.0	166	39%	.261
2018	LAN	MLB	38	11	5	0	25	24	132^2	108	20	2.8	10.2	150	40%	.268
2019	LAN	MLB	39	4	1	0	13	13	58^2	48	10	2.8	11.0	72	52%	.275
2020	MIN	MLB	40	4	2	0	11	11	52	42	6	2.8	10.2	59	46%	.275

Comparables: Arthur Rhodes, Manny Parra, Mike Remlinger

Psycho Rich seems like a bizarre nickname for a guy who looks like any other suburban dad on first glance, but everything about his demeanor changes when he's scheduled to pitch—or when he's trying to enter Foxboro Stadium. That competitiveness on the field, along with his personality off the field, has endeared him to the organization, teammates, and fans alike. Due to knee and elbow issues, the oft-injured Hill only pitched about a third of the innings he'd have liked to, but was nonetheless effective when on the mound. After the season concluded, we found that he had to battle to pitch his final 6 2/3 innings due to a re-injured MCL in his knee and a detached UCL in his elbow that will cause him to miss at least half of next season. He gave up two runs and hit one double in that span. Soon to turn 40, his future is that of the Lakers in reverse as he'll leave behind the bright lights of L.A. for the polite tundra of Minnesota.

YEAR	TEAM	LVL	AGE	WHIP	ERA	DRA	WARP	MPH	FB%	WHF	CSP
2017	LAN	MLB	37	1.09	3.32	3.35	3.4	91.0	54.8	12.7	49.2
2018	LAN	MLB	38	1.12	3.66	3.92	2.1	91.6	58.8	11.6	54.5
2019	LAN	MLB	39	1.12	2.45	3.39	1.5	92.6	52.6	12.3	56.1
2020	MIN	MLB	40	1.11	3.13	3.30	1.3	90.0	54.1	11.8	52.1

Rich Hill, continued

Pitch Shape vs LHH

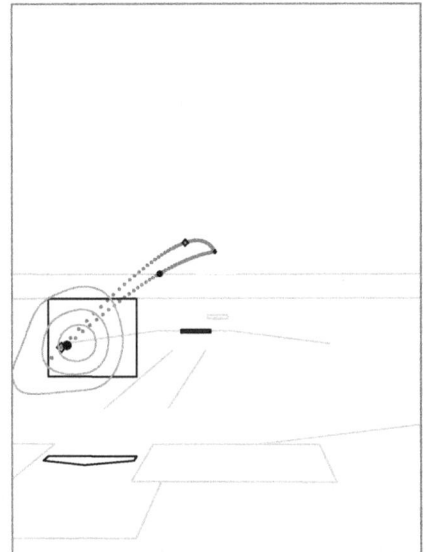

Pitch Shape vs RHH

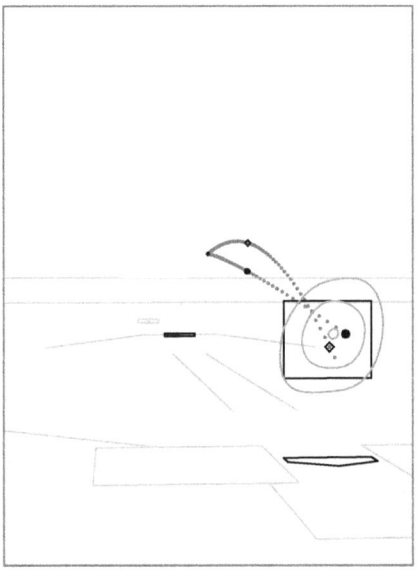

Type	Frequency	Velocity	H Movement	V Movement
● Fastball	52.0%	90.8 [95]	9.7 [87]	-13.9 [105]
☐ Sinker				
+ Cutter				
▲ Changeup				
✕ Splitter				
▽ Slider				
◇ Curveball	45.8%	74.6 [87]	-15.7 [133]	-57.5 [79]
✢ Slow Curveball				
✶ Knuckleball				
▼ Screwball				

Minnesota Twins 2020

Zack Littell RHP
Born: 10/05/95 Age: 24 Bats: R Throws: R
Height: 6'4" Weight: 220 Origin: Round 11, 2013 Draft (#327 overall)

YEAR	TEAM	LVL	AGE	W	L	SV	G	GS	IP	H	HR	BB/9	K/9	K	GB%	BABIP
2017	TAM	A+	21	9	1	0	13	11	71^1	65	4	1.9	7.2	57	55%	.302
2017	TRN	AA	21	5	0	0	7	7	44	37	3	1.6	10.6	52	52%	.304
2017	CHT	AA	21	5	0	0	7	7	41^2	33	1	3.9	7.1	33	55%	.274
2018	CHT	AA	22	0	3	0	5	5	23	28	3	2.7	12.5	32	38%	.431
2018	ROC	AAA	22	6	6	0	19	15	106	100	5	3.4	8.3	98	40%	.310
2018	MIN	MLB	22	0	2	0	8	2	20^1	25	3	4.9	6.2	14	44%	.319
2019	ROC	AAA	23	3	3	1	20	7	63	55	11	3.6	9.7	68	49%	.278
2019	MIN	MLB	23	6	0	0	29	0	37	34	4	2.2	7.8	32	39%	.297
2020	MIN	MLB	24	2	2	0	44	0	46	47	6	3.3	8.1	42	42%	.304

Comparables: Robert Gsellman, Jake Thompson, Touki Toussaint

Littell rode a mix-master profile to the majors in 2018, leaning on arsenal depth rather than any overwhelming quality to force an audition in a swing role. That didn't go well, so he consolidated things into a tidy fastball-slider package for his encore and provided a sneaky chunk of consistent value as an emergent middle man. Outside of taking an eight-run lump for the team in late May, he yielded just three earned runs in 28 appearances. The view under his hood painted a bit of a lucky picture: he didn't strike out a ton of batters, and when opponents made contact they tended to square 'em up at an uncomfortable rate. Still, he'll pitch as a 24-year-old for the entirety of 2020, and his breakout performance and remaining option should make him a valuable piece of the 40-man puzzle.

YEAR	TEAM	LVL	AGE	WHIP	ERA	DRA	WARP	MPH	FB%	WHF	CSP
2017	TAM	A+	21	1.12	1.77	3.61	1.4				
2017	TRN	AA	21	1.02	2.05	3.35	1.0				
2017	CHT	AA	21	1.22	2.81	4.32	0.4				
2018	CHT	AA	22	1.52	5.87	5.36	0.0				
2018	ROC	AAA	22	1.32	3.57	4.26	1.5				
2018	MIN	MLB	22	1.77	6.20	6.71	-0.4	94.8	58.5	8	49.2
2019	ROC	AAA	23	1.27	3.71	3.32	2.0				
2019	MIN	MLB	23	1.16	2.68	5.42	0.0	96.4	49.1	14.4	50.7
2020	MIN	MLB	24	1.39	4.78	4.71	0.2	95.7	54.3	12.3	51.5

Zack Littell, continued

Pitch Shape vs LHH

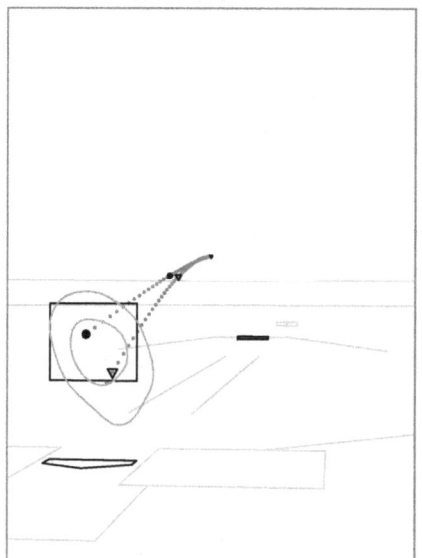

Pitch Shape vs RHH

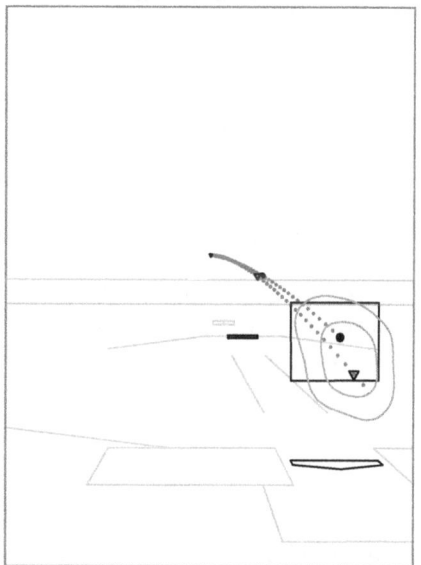

Type	Frequency	Velocity	H Movement	V Movement
● Fastball	48.7%	94 [105]	-6.9 [100]	-13.9 [105]
☐ Sinker				
+ Cutter				
▲ Changeup				
✕ Splitter				
▽ Slider	49.1%	86.7 [110]	0.8 [83]	-27.7 [116]
◇ Curveball				
✦ Slow Curveball				
✳ Knuckleball				
▼ Screwball				

Minnesota Twins 2020

Kenta Maeda   RHP

Born: 04/11/88   Age: 32   Bats: R   Throws: R
Height: 6'1"   Weight: 184   Origin: International Free Agent, 2016

YEAR	TEAM	LVL	AGE	W	L	SV	G	GS	IP	H	HR	BB/9	K/9	K	GB%	BABIP
2017	LAN	MLB	29	13	6	1	29	25	134[1]	121	22	2.3	9.4	140	40%	.278
2018	LAN	MLB	30	8	10	2	39	20	125[1]	115	13	3.1	11.0	153	42%	.321
2019	LAN	MLB	31	10	8	3	37	26	153[2]	114	22	3.0	9.9	169	41%	.243
2020	LAN	MLB	32	10	7	0	44	23	143	118	22	3.0	10.2	162	41%	.274

Comparables: Robb Nen, Eric Gagne, John Wetteland

Maeda's story in the majors has been essentially the same every year now. He spends most of the year as an average starter before converting to relief to patch an otherwise leaky bullpen. It's recently emerged that Maeda is tired of that cycle and it's hard to blame him; a significant portion of his contract is based on incentives awarded for innings accumulated and starts made. It's hard to do those things when one's time in the rotation is cut short each year. For that reason though, the Dodgers are unlikely to change much in regards to Maeda's seasonal pattern. The Dodgers are unlikely to trade him, so the only way for Maeda to change his future is to ensure he is one of their three starters come playoff time. While somewhat unlikely, it's definitely possible because his problem is clear: he dominates righties (.590 OPS) and struggles against lefties (.766 OPS). Maeda has the stuff to handle the split as his changeup is a plus offering, but he's never been able to do it consistently. Until he does, it's difficult to predict a different story for him in 2020.

YEAR	TEAM	LVL	AGE	WHIP	ERA	DRA	WARP	MPH	FB%	WHF	CSP
2017	LAN	MLB	29	1.15	4.22	3.53	3.0	93.5	43.4	13	47.1
2018	LAN	MLB	30	1.26	3.81	2.78	3.6	93.9	44.4	15.8	46.1
2019	LAN	MLB	31	1.07	4.04	3.28	4.1	93.8	37.3	15.7	45.4
2020	LAN	MLB	32	1.17	3.17	3.57	3.4	92.8	40.5	14.9	45.6

Kenta Maeda, continued

Pitch Shape vs LHH	Pitch Shape vs RHH
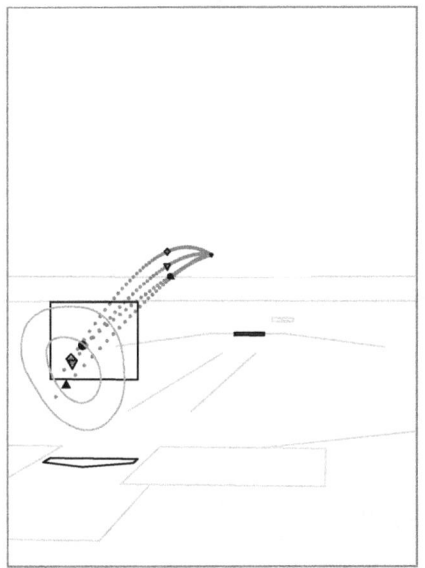	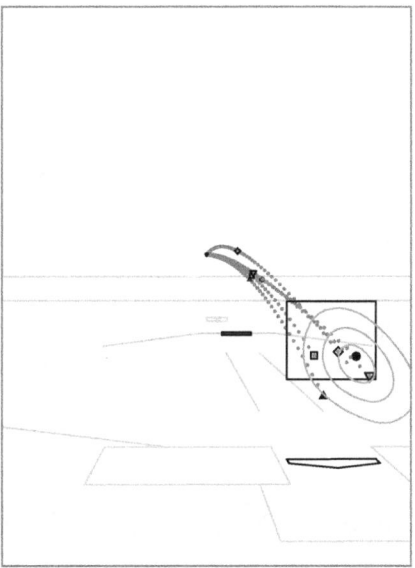

Type	Frequency	Velocity	H Movement	V Movement
● Fastball	34.1%	92.3 [100]	-5.6 [106]	-15 [103]
☐ Sinker	3.2%	91.9 [96]	-12.6 [100]	-20.6 [99]
+ Cutter				
▲ Changeup	23.8%	85.1 [99]	-10.4 [104]	-29.8 [93]
✕ Splitter				
▽ Slider	31.5%	83.7 [97]	4.6 [98]	-29.4 [111]
◇ Curveball	7.4%	77.2 [95]	10.3 [112]	-51.2 [92]
⊕ Slow Curveball				
✳ Knuckleball				
▼ Screwball				

Minnesota Twins 2020

Trevor May RHP
Born: 09/23/89   Age: 30   Bats: R   Throws: R
Height: 6'5"   Weight: 240   Origin: Round 4, 2008 Draft (#136 overall)

YEAR	TEAM	LVL	AGE	W	L	SV	G	GS	IP	H	HR	BB/9	K/9	K	GB%	BABIP
2018	ROC	AAA	28	0	4	2	13	4	27	24	2	5.3	8.3	25	40%	.293
2018	MIN	MLB	28	4	1	3	24	1	25^1	21	4	1.8	12.8	36	41%	.298
2019	MIN	MLB	29	5	3	2	65	0	64^1	43	8	3.6	11.1	79	35%	.233
2020	MIN	MLB	30	3	3	4	60	0	64	56	9	3.8	10.9	77	36%	.296

Comparables: Jeremy Jeffress, Neftalí Feliz, Bobby Parnell

Last year in this space we suggested May lean a little less on a heretofore pedestrian fastball. Rather than listen to our advice, he instead went out and made his fastball better. Another year removed from a surgeon's knife, his velocity ticked up to touch 96 mph. Some in-season fiddling with his slider fueled a breakout effort— with that pitch and, accordingly, his pitching at large. By the second half May had morphed into the setup monster Minnesota needed. He'll be in line for a nice free-agent payday if he can repeat his efforts this season.

YEAR	TEAM	LVL	AGE	WHIP	ERA	DRA	WARP	MPH	FB%	WHF	CSP
2018	ROC	AAA	28	1.48	4.00	4.45	0.3				
2018	MIN	MLB	28	1.03	3.20	2.98	0.6	95.7	59.2	15.6	46.7
2019	MIN	MLB	29	1.07	2.94	3.95	1.0	97.6	62.9	13.9	46.3
2020	MIN	MLB	30	1.30	4.14	4.16	0.7	96.4	61.8	14.3	46.3

Trevor May, continued

Pitch Shape vs LHH

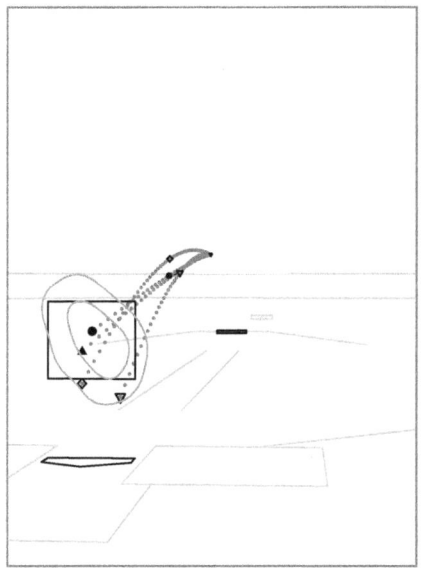

Pitch Shape vs RHH

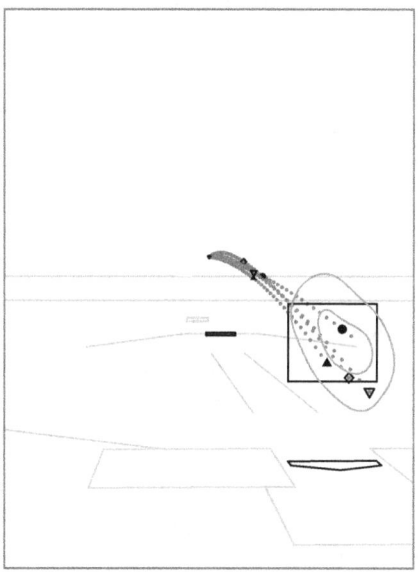

Type	Frequency	Velocity	H Movement	V Movement
● Fastball	62.9%	96 [110]	-4.6 [110]	-12.5 [109]
☐ Sinker				
+ Cutter				
▲ Changeup	10.0%	87.9 [110]	-10.1 [105]	-19.6 [123]
✕ Splitter				
▽ Slider	10.9%	84.3 [99]	5.4 [102]	-37.8 [86]
◇ Curveball	16.2%	80.4 [106]	8.6 [104]	-47.4 [100]
⊕ Slow Curveball				
✱ Knuckleball				
▼ Screwball				

Minnesota Twins 2020

Jake Odorizzi   RHP
Born: 03/27/90   Age: 30   Bats: R   Throws: R
Height: 6'2"   Weight: 190   Origin: Round 1, 2008 Draft (#32 overall)

YEAR	TEAM	LVL	AGE	W	L	SV	G	GS	IP	H	HR	BB/9	K/9	K	GB%	BABIP
2017	TBA	MLB	27	10	8	0	28	28	143^1	117	30	3.8	8.0	127	32%	.227
2018	MIN	MLB	28	7	10	0	32	32	164^1	151	20	3.8	8.9	162	31%	.290
2019	MIN	MLB	29	15	7	0	30	30	159	139	16	3.0	10.1	178	37%	.302
2020	MIN	MLB	30	11	8	0	28	28	149	138	24	3.4	9.8	162	35%	.295

Comparables: Kevin Gausman, Ubaldo Jiménez, Enyel De Los Santos

Odorizzi is the poster child for both: adaptive analytics and the terrifying prospect of free agency in the year 2020. After seeking out restructured training and strategic approaches at a Florida performance institute last winter, Odorizzi added a couple ticks to his fastball and worked a little farther down in the zone. His performance with the pitch improved. Better gas was accompanied by a splitter that featured more drop than usual, which helped him rein in his longball tendencies, and permitted him to put together the kind of solidly above-average walk year that should absolutely get a 30-year-old mid-rotation starter paid. Alas, the poisoned waters of the free market kept him in Minnesota as he accepted the qualifying offer. He'll make his play for a multi-year deal next winter instead.

YEAR	TEAM	LVL	AGE	WHIP	ERA	DRA	WARP	MPH	FB%	WHF	CSP
2017	TBA	MLB	27	1.24	4.14	5.29	0.5	93.8	48.7	12.1	43.9
2018	MIN	MLB	28	1.34	4.49	5.62	-0.6	92.9	54.3	11.7	42.1
2019	MIN	MLB	29	1.21	3.51	4.23	2.7	94.6	57.8	13.8	45.4
2020	MIN	MLB	30	1.30	4.32	4.33	2.0	93.1	54.2	12.6	43.8

Jake Odorizzi, continued

Pitch Shape vs LHH

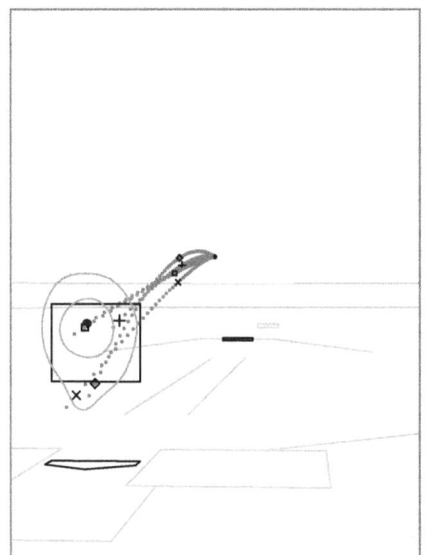

Pitch Shape vs RHH

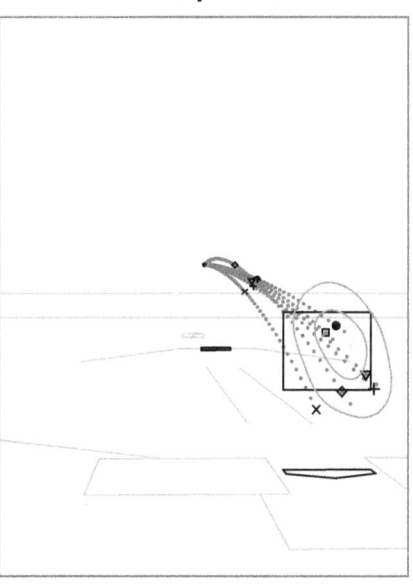

Type	Frequency	Velocity	H Movement	V Movement
● Fastball	37.5%	93 [102]	-8.1 [95]	-13.2 [107]
□ Sinker	20.2%	93.3 [104]	-11.1 [110]	-14.6 [120]
+ Cutter	8.5%	86.9 [89]	4.3 [115]	-24.5 [98]
▲ Changeup				
× Splitter	17.0%	85.3 [101]	-9.8 [93]	-28.2 [103]
▽ Slider	10.3%	84.8 [102]	5.6 [103]	-29 [112]
◇ Curveball	6.5%	75.7 [90]	8.1 [103]	-53.1 [88]
⊕ Slow Curveball				
✳ Knuckleball				
▼ Screwball				

Minnesota Twins 2020

Michael Pineda   RHP
Born: 01/18/89   Age: 31   Bats: R   Throws: R
Height: 6'7"   Weight: 280   Origin: International Free Agent, 2005

YEAR	TEAM	LVL	AGE	W	L	SV	G	GS	IP	H	HR	BB/9	K/9	K	GB%	BABIP
2017	NYA	MLB	28	8	4	0	17	17	96¹	103	20	2.0	8.6	92	52%	.302
2018	FTM	A+	29	0	0	0	2	2	6	7	0	0.0	6.0	4	35%	.350
2019	MIN	MLB	30	11	5	0	26	26	146	141	23	1.7	8.6	140	37%	.292
2020	MIN	MLB	31	7	5	0	18	18	100	96	17	2.2	8.9	99	39%	.292

Comparables: Brett Anderson, Ricky Nolasco, Tyson Ross

The recipient of a two-year deal on the front end of Tommy John recovery last winter, Pineda returned to the bump and more or less picked up where he'd left off. He threw a higher percentage of changeups in Minnesota than he'd ever thrown before, and he managed good results with the pitch, even seeing a jump in fastball effectiveness despite coming back from the knife with lighter velocity. Somewhere along the way he lost the feel for his slider, but it didn't seem to matter as his game remained the same: limited baserunners, loud contact and a wobbly relationship with Lady Luck. As the calendar flipped to September he found himself on pace for a solid season in the middle of a playoff-bound rotation. That's when it all came crashing down, as it turned out that his comeback performance had been at least partially bought and paid for by a banned diuretic. His season-ending suspension cost him the shine of October's lights and a healthier paycheck. Still, the Twins liked what they saw when they did see it, and it all sounded so nice they played twice, signing him to another two-year deal over the winter.

YEAR	TEAM	LVL	AGE	WHIP	ERA	DRA	WARP	MPH	FB%	WHF	CSP
2017	NYA	MLB	28	1.29	4.39	3.36	2.4	96.2	48.5	13.3	46.6
2018	FTM	A+	29	1.17	1.50	5.67	0.0				
2019	MIN	MLB	30	1.16	4.01	4.74	1.6	95.1	55.6	13.4	49
2020	MIN	MLB	31	1.21	4.16	4.30	1.4	94.6	53.2	13.3	47.8

Michael Pineda, continued

Pitch Shape vs LHH

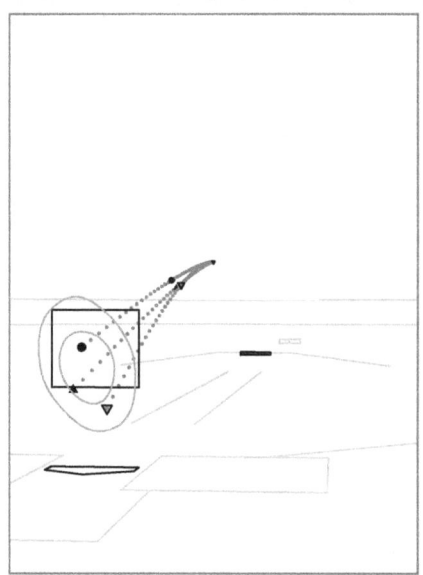

Pitch Shape vs RHH

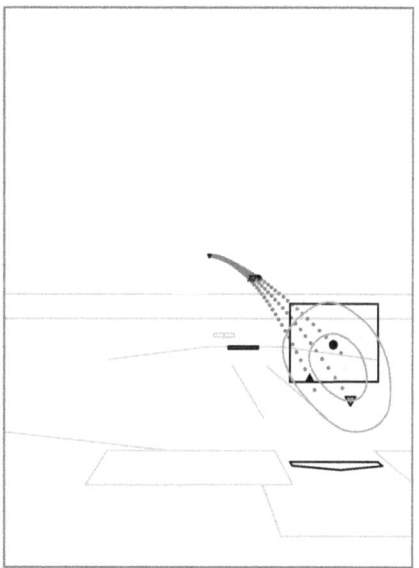

Type	Frequency	Velocity	H Movement	V Movement
● Fastball	55.5%	92.9 [101]	-5.2 [107]	-16.4 [99]
☐ Sinker				
+ Cutter				
▲ Changeup	15.2%	87.5 [108]	-13.3 [90]	-24.6 [108]
✕ Splitter				
▽ Slider	29.2%	84.2 [99]	-0.9 [75]	-33.2 [100]
◇ Curveball				
⊕ Slow Curveball				
✻ Knuckleball				
▼ Screwball				

Minnesota Twins 2020

Taylor Rogers LHP

Born: 12/17/90   Age: 29   Bats: L   Throws: L
Height: 6'3"   Weight: 190   Origin: Round 11, 2012 Draft (#340 overall)

YEAR	TEAM	LVL	AGE	W	L	SV	G	GS	IP	H	HR	BB/9	K/9	K	GB%	BABIP
2017	MIN	MLB	26	7	3	0	69	0	55^2	52	6	3.4	7.9	49	46%	.291
2018	MIN	MLB	27	1	2	2	72	0	68^1	49	3	2.1	9.9	75	46%	.280
2019	MIN	MLB	28	2	4	30	60	0	69	58	8	1.4	11.7	90	53%	.307
2020	MIN	MLB	29	3	3	38	60	0	64	58	7	2.2	10.7	76	49%	.315

Comparables: Justin Grimm, Alex Young, Rafael Perez

It all came together for Rogers, as he completed his transformation from a former back-end control lefty, to a burgeoning LOOGY, to a dominant all-world reliever. The introduction of a slider in 2018 had fueled his breakout, and his work with pitching coach Wes Johnson resulted in another tick of fastball velocity to tie the whole package together. Righties and lefties struggled each struggled to find his stuff consistently at any point in the season, and he even got to check out his twin brother break into the bigs. It's been a fun rise for the former 11th-rounder, and he'll resume his role at the back end of the 'pen with another chance to rack up saves before entering an arbitration system that pays closers handsomely.

YEAR	TEAM	LVL	AGE	WHIP	ERA	DRA	WARP	MPH	FB%	WHF	CSP
2017	MIN	MLB	26	1.31	3.07	4.63	0.3	94.9	62.3	9.3	50
2018	MIN	MLB	27	0.95	2.63	3.33	1.3	95.2	52.9	12.3	51.5
2019	MIN	MLB	28	1.00	2.61	2.79	1.9	96.5	50.1	11.9	53.5
2020	MIN	MLB	29	1.16	3.29	3.42	1.2	95.0	53.7	11.4	51.9

Taylor Rogers, continued

Pitch Shape vs LHH

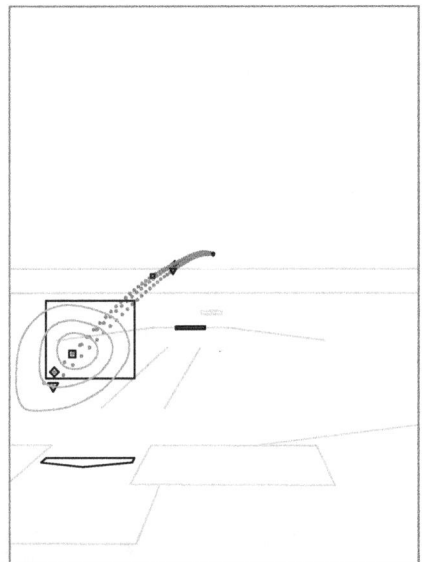

Pitch Shape vs RHH

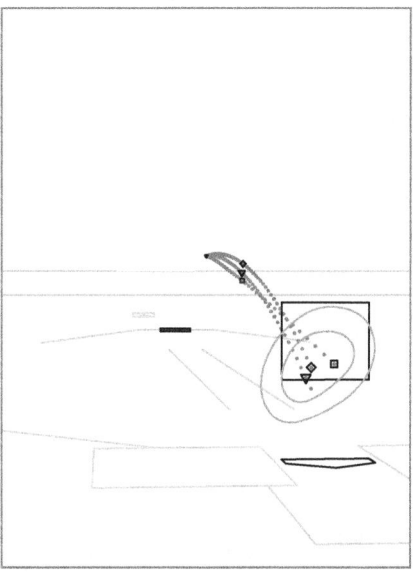

Type	Frequency	Velocity	H Movement	V Movement
● Fastball				
□ Sinker	50.0%	95.1 [113]	15.4 [82]	-20.7 [99]
+ Cutter				
▲ Changeup				
✕ Splitter				
▽ Slider	31.1%	83.3 [95]	-8.9 [116]	-32.5 [102]
◇ Curveball	18.8%	80.4 [106]	-11.7 [117]	-38.2 [120]
⊕ Slow Curveball				
✳ Knuckleball				
▼ Screwball				

Fernando Romero RHP

Born: 12/24/94   Age: 25   Bats: R   Throws: R
Height: 6'0"   Weight: 215   Origin: International Free Agent, 2011

YEAR	TEAM	LVL	AGE	W	L	SV	G	GS	IP	H	HR	BB/9	K/9	K	GB%	BABIP
2017	CHT	AA	22	11	9	0	24	23	125	124	4	3.2	8.6	120	54%	.328
2018	ROC	AAA	23	5	6	0	16	13	90²	85	5	3.2	6.8	69	50%	.294
2018	MIN	MLB	23	3	3	0	11	11	55²	60	6	3.1	7.3	45	48%	.318
2019	ROC	AAA	24	2	4	4	35	1	57²	53	7	4.5	9.8	63	63%	.311
2019	MIN	MLB	24	0	1	0	15	0	14	19	2	7.1	11.6	18	52%	.425
2020	MIN	MLB	25	2	2	0	33	0	35	35	5	4.2	8.5	33	54%	.306

Comparables: Duane Underwood Jr., Allen Webster, John Gant

Once a surefire rotation anchor in the making, Romero slid into a relief role last year as the club sought to harness his obscene stuff. The days changed but the song stayed the same, and he again stalled out against high-end hitters and failed to contribute meaningful innings to the big-league club. His 97-mph sinker and hard slider both miss a bunch of bats and get beat into the ground often, so it's far too early to give up on him. But he'll head into 2020 out of options, as a true wildcard for the Twins' pen planning.

YEAR	TEAM	LVL	AGE	WHIP	ERA	DRA	WARP	MPH	FB%	WHF	CSP
2017	CHT	AA	22	1.35	3.53	4.99	0.2				
2018	ROC	AAA	23	1.29	3.57	3.73	1.8				
2018	MIN	MLB	23	1.42	4.69	6.13	-0.5	97.5	63.3	11.3	48.4
2019	ROC	AAA	24	1.42	4.37	4.34	1.1				
2019	MIN	MLB	24	2.14	7.07	3.77	0.2	98.7	67.6	12.6	43.1
2020	MIN	MLB	25	1.47	5.04	4.85	0.1	97.5	66	11.9	46.5

Fernando Romero, continued

Pitch Shape vs LHH

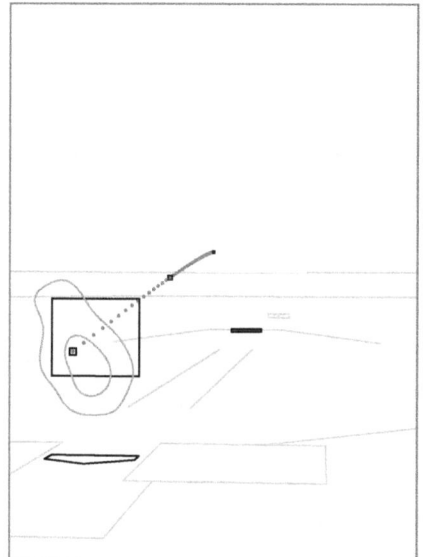

Pitch Shape vs RHH

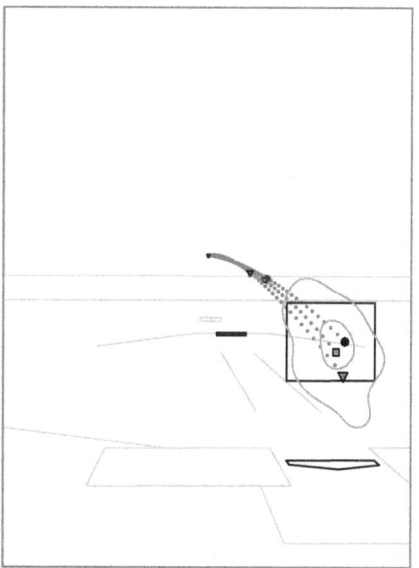

Type	Frequency	Velocity	H Movement	V Movement
● Fastball	17.3%	96.8 [112]	-12.2 [76]	-14.3 [104]
☐ Sinker	50.4%	97.3 [124]	-13.5 [94]	-16.9 [112]
+ Cutter				
▲ Changeup	3.6%	91.9 [124]	-13 [92]	-22.9 [113]
✕ Splitter				
▽ Slider	28.8%	87.5 [113]	2.8 [91]	-33.2 [100]
◇ Curveball				
⊕ Slow Curveball				
✳ Knuckleball				
▼ Screwball				

Sergio Romo   RHP

Born: 03/04/83   Age: 37   Bats: R   Throws: R
Height: 5'11"   Weight: 185   Origin: Round 28, 2005 Draft (#852 overall)

YEAR	TEAM	LVL	AGE	W	L	SV	G	GS	IP	H	HR	BB/9	K/9	K	GB%	BABIP
2017	LAN	MLB	34	1	1	0	30	0	25	23	7	4.3	11.2	31	35%	.276
2017	TBA	MLB	34	2	0	0	25	0	30²	19	2	2.1	8.2	28	40%	.218
2018	TBA	MLB	35	3	4	25	73	5	67¹	65	11	2.7	10.0	75	38%	.309
2019	MIA	MLB	36	2	0	17	38	0	37²	33	4	3.1	7.9	33	36%	.274
2019	MIN	MLB	36	0	1	3	27	0	22²	17	3	1.6	10.7	27	37%	.246
2020	MIN	MLB	37	3	3	5	55	0	58	50	12	2.7	9.6	62	37%	.264

Comparables: Trevor Hoffman, Tom Henke, Joakim Soria

A few years back psychology professor Frank Durgin ran a study about human perceptions of hill slant. He found (overwhelmingly) that younger, less experienced people tended to wildly exaggerate the angle of a steep hill, while his sample of older, more experienced participants made much more educated, accurate estimates. Wisdom comes from experience. Usually, humans apply the wisdom of our experiences to make adjustments and offset the decay of our physical skills and the degradation of our brain's processing speed as we age; most of us consolidate our strengths in order to overcome our growing weaknesses. And then there are the people who just never learn or grow or change in any way. Sometimes those people become President of the United States. Other times they throw a dozen seasons of excellent high-leverage relief in the major leagues.

An ugly April and some shaky control in May briefly jeopardized an impressive streak of career-long above-average (or better) DRA performance, but Romo just kept flipping sliders throughout a much more stable midsummer that eventually saw him closing games in Miami. He was really good against lefties in 2019, and that's a good thing to be when you're a free agent who'll be 37 on Opening Day. It's an uphill climb indeed to hold onto a bullpen seat at that age, but being able to spin it like Romo does makes that path a little less steep.

YEAR	TEAM	LVL	AGE	WHIP	ERA	DRA	WARP	MPH	FB%	WHF	CSP
2017	LAN	MLB	34	1.40	6.12	2.58	0.7	88.2	27.2	15.4	41.1
2017	TBA	MLB	34	0.85	1.47	3.76	0.5	87.9	41.5	16.3	41.7
2018	TBA	MLB	35	1.26	4.14	2.80	1.7	88.1	30.1	14.6	44
2019	MIA	MLB	36	1.22	3.58	5.76	-0.2	87.6	26.2	15	42.7
2019	MIN	MLB	36	0.93	3.18	2.73	0.6	87.5	22	14.6	40.5
2020	MIN	MLB	37	1.17	3.96	4.16	0.7	86.5	28.1	14.6	41.4

Sergio Romo, continued

Pitch Shape vs LHH

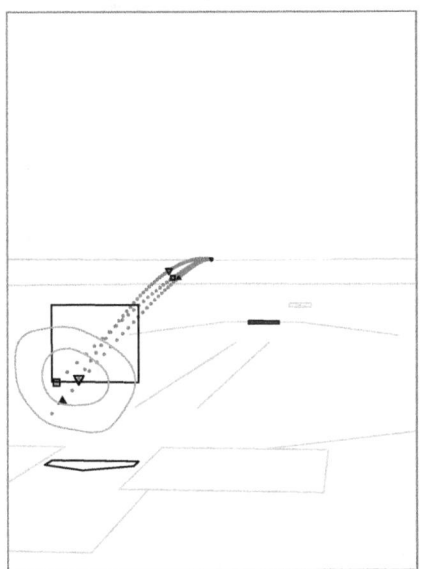

Pitch Shape vs RHH

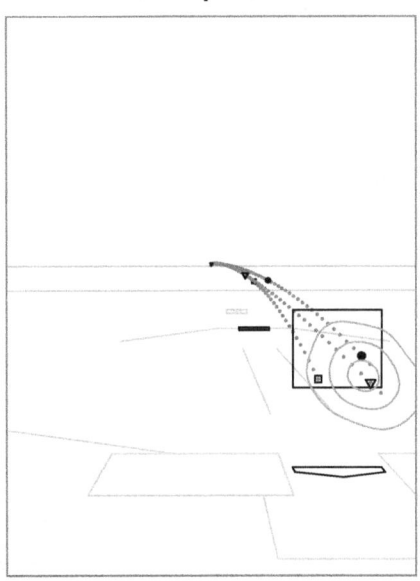

Type	Frequency	Velocity	H Movement	V Movement
● Fastball	9.3%	86.7 [84]	-11.7 [78]	-22.3 [83]
☐ Sinker	15.1%	86.4 [68]	-16.2 [77]	-30.5 [64]
+ Cutter				
▲ Changeup	16.0%	80.4 [82]	-17.4 [71]	-36.2 [74]
✕ Splitter				
▽ Slider	59.6%	77.6 [71]	13.4 [135]	-33.7 [98]
◇ Curveball				
⊕ Slow Curveball				
✳ Knuckleball				
▼ Screwball				

Devin Smeltzer LHP

Born: 09/07/95   Age: 24   Bats: R   Throws: L
Height: 6'3"   Weight: 195   Origin: Round 5, 2016 Draft (#161 overall)

YEAR	TEAM	LVL	AGE	W	L	SV	G	GS	IP	H	HR	BB/9	K/9	K	GB%	BABIP
2017	GRL	A	21	2	3	0	10	10	52[1]	40	6	2.1	9.8	57	49%	.266
2017	RCU	A+	21	5	4	0	16	15	90	107	10	1.8	10.2	102	44%	.367
2018	TUL	AA	22	5	5	0	23	14	83[2]	94	9	2.0	7.2	67	39%	.321
2018	CHT	AA	22	0	0	4	10	0	12	14	0	1.5	12.0	16	36%	.389
2019	PEN	AA	23	3	1	0	5	5	30	19	0	0.9	9.9	33	42%	.268
2019	ROC	AAA	23	1	4	0	15	14	74[1]	68	14	2.3	8.6	71	40%	.271
2019	MIN	MLB	23	2	2	1	11	6	49	50	8	2.2	7.0	38	39%	.294
2020	MIN	MLB	24	4	4	0	11	11	60	66	12	2.7	7.0	46	38%	.297

Comparables: Josh Rogers, Ranger Suárez, Andrew Heaney

Smeltzer flew a curious course in his big-league debut as that rare left-hander who gets tuned up by his own kind. It wasn't a wholly surprising outcome: he'd dabbled in reverse-splitting at points in his minor-league career, and loitered around even at other times. His curveball too often strayed from its intended target, meeting barrels instead of mitts. Nonetheless, Smeltzer has a three-pitch mix that also includes a dandy of a changeup. He should remain useful in the majors—and he might even prove to be an asset if he can figure out how to retire lefties.

YEAR	TEAM	LVL	AGE	WHIP	ERA	DRA	WARP	MPH	FB%	WHF	CSP
2017	GRL	A	21	0.99	3.78	2.93	1.4				
2017	RCU	A+	21	1.39	4.40	4.75	0.5				
2018	TUL	AA	22	1.35	4.73	4.70	0.5				
2018	CHT	AA	22	1.33	3.00	3.60	0.2				
2019	PEN	AA	23	0.73	0.60	2.66	0.8				
2019	ROC	AAA	23	1.17	3.63	3.89	2.0				
2019	MIN	MLB	23	1.27	3.86	5.59	0.0	90.9	45.8	10.2	49.3
2020	MIN	MLB	24	1.40	5.41	5.33	0.2	90.7	47.1	10.6	50.8

Devin Smeltzer, continued

Pitch Shape vs LHH

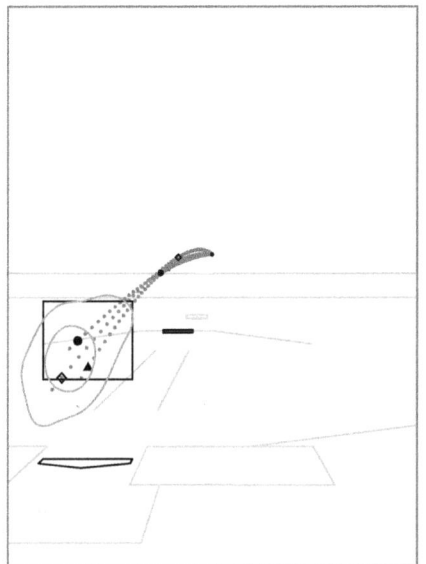

Pitch Shape vs RHH

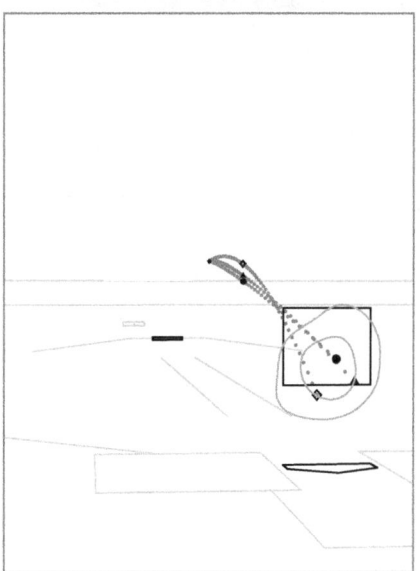

Type	Frequency	Velocity	H Movement	V Movement
● Fastball	45.8%	89.1 [91]	9.5 [88]	-16.6 [98]
☐ Sinker				
+ Cutter				
▲ Changeup	25.5%	82.8 [91]	12.9 [92]	-31.8 [87]
✕ Splitter				
▽ Slider	4.2%	82.9 [94]	-3.7 [95]	-31.4 [105]
◇ Curveball	24.5%	76.8 [94]	-10.8 [113]	-50.5 [94]
⊕ Slow Curveball				
✳ Knuckleball				
▼ Screwball				

Cody Stashak RHP

Born: 06/04/94 Age: 26 Bats: R Throws: R
Height: 6'2" Weight: 169 Origin: Round 13, 2015 Draft (#380 overall)

YEAR	TEAM	LVL	AGE	W	L	SV	G	GS	IP	H	HR	BB/9	K/9	K	GB%	BABIP
2017	FTM	A+	23	3	4	0	16	16	83^1	72	7	2.2	7.8	72	33%	.279
2017	CHT	AA	23	0	0	0	3	0	6	4	0	0.0	15.0	10	17%	.333
2018	CHT	AA	24	1	1	4	35	2	55^2	47	4	2.1	11.2	69	32%	.321
2019	PEN	AA	25	2	3	4	19	0	28^1	28	4	1.6	12.7	40	30%	.348
2019	ROC	AAA	25	5	0	0	14	2	25	17	1	1.4	12.2	34	41%	.276
2019	MIN	MLB	25	0	1	0	18	1	25	29	3	0.4	9.0	25	25%	.351
2020	MIN	MLB	26	2	2	0	33	0	35	32	6	2.3	9.8	38	30%	.287

Comparables: Adbert Alzolay, Wei-Chieh Huang, Tyler Wilson

A former 13th-round pick by way of Queens, Stashak makes this year's Annual after missing the cut last year. That'll happen when a pitcher whiffs eight for every walk he issues in the high minors, then goes out and drops a 25-to-1 ratio in his big-league stint. He doesn't throw a particularly fast fastball, but it plays up with sneakiness generated by his extension and backspin. His slider's a short little thing that off of barrels, and his mechanics are cleaner than any Dirty Money radio edit, too. He's an interesting candidate to fill a Yusmeiro Petit-like hybrid role as soon as 2020.

YEAR	TEAM	LVL	AGE	WHIP	ERA	DRA	WARP	MPH	FB%	WHF	CSP
2017	FTM	A+	23	1.10	3.89	3.62	1.6				
2017	CHT	AA	23	0.67	0.00	2.55	0.2				
2018	CHT	AA	24	1.08	2.75	3.42	1.0				
2019	PEN	AA	25	1.16	4.76	5.23	-0.2				
2019	ROC	AAA	25	0.84	1.44	2.29	1.0				
2019	MIN	MLB	25	1.20	3.24	5.85	-0.1	93.0	54	18	54.3
2020	MIN	MLB	26	1.17	4.00	4.15	0.4	92.6	54.9	18.3	55.3

Cody Stashak, continued

Pitch Shape vs LHH

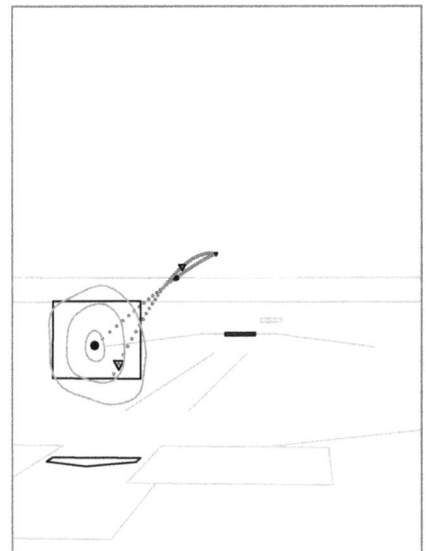

Pitch Shape vs RHH

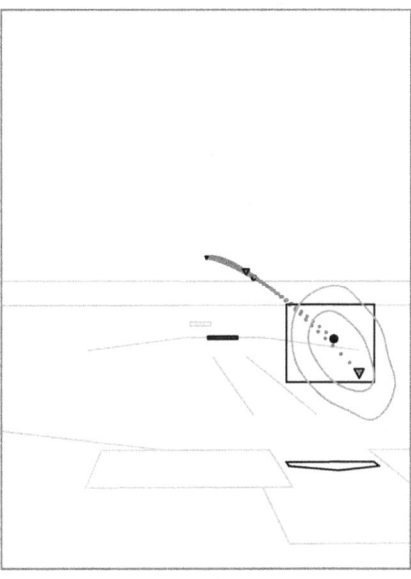

Type	Frequency	Velocity	H Movement	V Movement
● Fastball	54.0%	91.7 [98]	-3.8 [114]	-12.4 [109]
☐ Sinker				
+ Cutter				
▲ Changeup	7.1%	85.2 [100]	-8.1 [114]	-23.3 [112]
✕ Splitter				
▽ Slider	39.0%	82.1 [90]	8.8 [116]	-31.2 [105]
◇ Curveball				
⊕ Slow Curveball				
✳ Knuckleball				
▼ Screwball				

Lewis Thorpe LHP

Born: 11/23/95   Age: 24   Bats: R   Throws: L
Height: 6'1"   Weight: 218   Origin: International Free Agent, 2012

YEAR	TEAM	LVL	AGE	W	L	SV	G	GS	IP	H	HR	BB/9	K/9	K	GB%	BABIP
2017	FTM	A+	21	3	4	0	16	15	77	62	3	3.6	9.8	84	39%	.304
2017	CHT	AA	21	1	0	0	1	1	6	5	2	3.0	10.5	7	19%	.214
2018	CHT	AA	22	8	4	0	22	21	108	105	13	2.5	10.9	131	38%	.327
2018	ROC	AAA	22	0	3	0	4	4	21^2	20	3	2.5	10.8	26	45%	.321
2019	ROC	AAA	23	5	4	0	20	19	96^1	91	13	2.3	11.1	119	43%	.318
2019	MIN	MLB	23	3	2	0	12	2	27^2	38	3	3.3	10.1	31	35%	.438
2020	MIN	MLB	24	4	3	0	30	8	64	60	9	3.0	8.7	62	38%	.289

Comparables: Anthony Banda, Jake Odorizzi, Zack Littell

To label last season a success for Thorpe is to undersell it. The Aussie had previously lost two years of development to Tommy John surgery and recovery, as well as assorted complications therefrom. But, less than three years after his return to the bump, he found the rubber in Minnesota for a dozen appearances. Thorpe works across three velocity bands with a four-pitch mix, and has shown consistent, high-end strikeout ability throughout his minor-league career. That held true in his big-league debut, even if the results didn't. A couple clunkers in an unfamiliar relief role won't diminish the clear triumph of a fought-for debut, and he'll enter 2020 in line for a step up in quantity and quality.

YEAR	TEAM	LVL	AGE	WHIP	ERA	DRA	WARP	MPH	FB%	WHF	CSP
2017	FTM	A+	21	1.21	2.69	4.02	1.1				
2017	CHT	AA	21	1.17	6.00	4.12	0.1				
2018	CHT	AA	22	1.25	3.58	4.14	1.5				
2018	ROC	AAA	22	1.20	3.32	3.94	0.4				
2019	ROC	AAA	23	1.20	4.58	3.53	2.9				
2019	MIN	MLB	23	1.73	6.18	5.36	0.0	93.7	50	13.2	48.9
2020	MIN	MLB	24	1.28	4.15	4.20	0.9	93.5	51.5	13.6	50.4

Lewis Thorpe, continued

Pitch Shape vs LHH

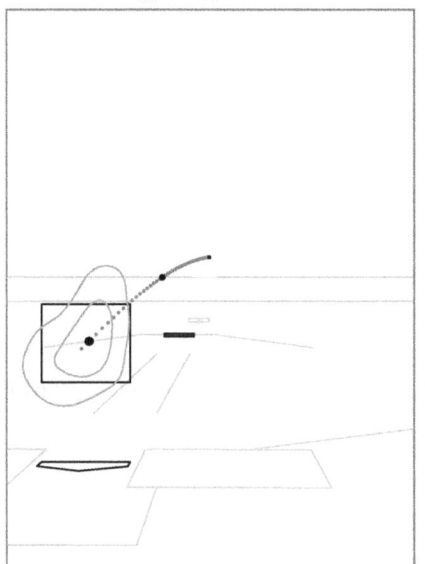

Pitch Shape vs RHH

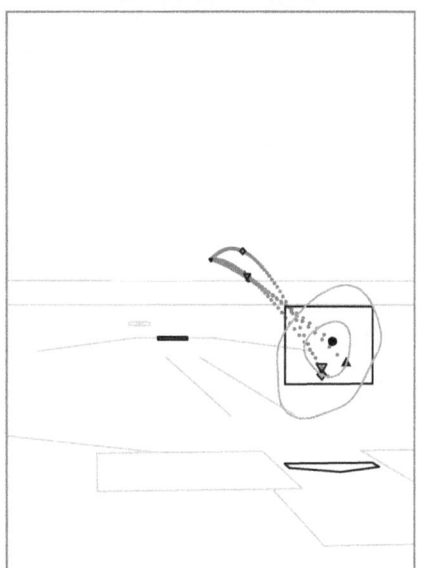

Type	Frequency	Velocity	H Movement	V Movement
● Fastball	50.0%	91.4 [97]	7.3 [98]	-14.6 [103]
☐ Sinker				
+ Cutter				
▲ Changeup	11.8%	84.4 [97]	10.1 [105]	-25.7 [105]
✕ Splitter				
▽ Slider	22.4%	84.1 [99]	-3.4 [93]	-30.5 [107]
◇ Curveball	15.9%	73.8 [84]	-8.8 [105]	-59.7 [74]
⊕ Slow Curveball				
✱ Knuckleball				
▼ Screwball				

Matt Wisler RHP

Born: 09/12/92 Age: 27 Bats: R Throws: R
Height: 6'3" Weight: 215 Origin: Round 7, 2011 Draft (#233 overall)

YEAR	TEAM	LVL	AGE	W	L	SV	G	GS	IP	H	HR	BB/9	K/9	K	GB%	BABIP
2017	GWN	AAA	24	7	5	0	18	14	93²	101	7	1.9	6.1	64	44%	.310
2017	ATL	MLB	24	0	1	0	20	1	32¹	43	5	3.6	6.1	22	33%	.342
2018	GWN	AAA	25	4	4	0	13	13	70	79	6	1.8	8.4	65	48%	.348
2018	LOU	AAA	25	1	1	0	8	2	19²	19	0	1.4	9.6	21	36%	.339
2018	ATL	MLB	25	1	1	0	7	3	26²	30	6	1.7	7.1	21	28%	.300
2018	CIN	MLB	25	0	0	0	11	0	13¹	11	2	1.4	7.4	11	42%	.231
2019	SEA	MLB	26	1	2	0	23	8	22¹	22	5	2.4	11.7	29	27%	.309
2019	SDN	MLB	26	2	2	0	21	0	29	34	5	3.1	10.6	34	46%	.363
2020	MIN	MLB	27	2	2	0	27	5	28	28	5	2.7	9.2	29	36%	.299

Comparables: Erasmo Ramírez, Archie Bradley, Vin Mazzaro

Wisler is on a quest to become the first slider-only pitcher in baseball, hucking it 70 percent of the time in 2019. It's a good hard slider, a variant on the cutter-dominant approaches of other relievers, but it hasn't reflected in the ERA yet, primarily because he's a fly ball pitcher who gives up a lot of home runs on fly balls. The pieces are interesting, however, and you can see why Minnesota wanted a chance to try to put them together.

YEAR	TEAM	LVL	AGE	WHIP	ERA	DRA	WARP	MPH	FB%	WHF	CSP
2017	GWN	AAA	24	1.29	3.56	4.74	1.0				
2017	ATL	MLB	24	1.73	8.35	7.24	-0.7	94.9	55.9	10.1	46.1
2018	GWN	AAA	25	1.33	4.37	4.73	0.6				
2018	LOU	AAA	25	1.12	1.83	5.65	0.0				
2018	ATL	MLB	25	1.31	5.40	3.99	0.3	94.9	53.4	10.2	49.5
2018	CIN	MLB	25	0.98	2.03	4.26	0.1	94.0	42.1	12.2	51.2
2019	SEA	MLB	26	1.25	6.04	4.54	0.2	94.5	29.8	14.9	44.8
2019	SDN	MLB	26	1.52	5.28	3.86	0.5	94.9	28.6	16.2	47.8
2020	MIN	MLB	27	1.28	4.38	4.45	0.2	94.2	40.5	13.4	48.1

Matt Wisler, continued

Pitch Shape vs LHH

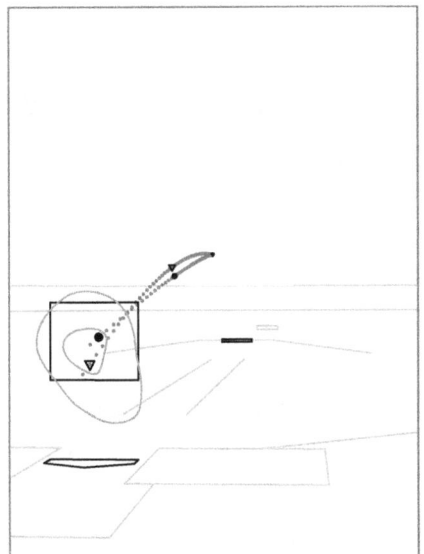

Pitch Shape vs RHH

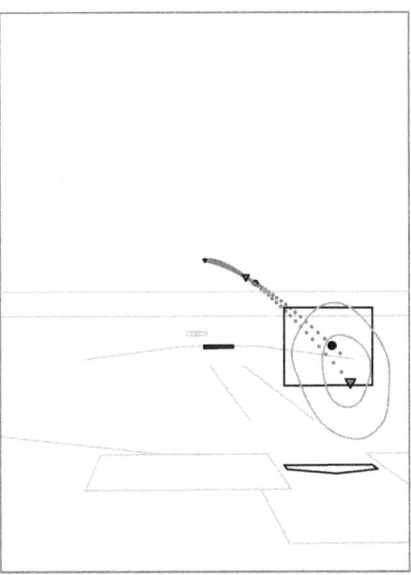

Type	Frequency	Velocity	H Movement	V Movement
● Fastball	27.5%	93.1 [102]	-5.7 [105]	-13.5 [106]
☐ Sinker				
+ Cutter				
▲ Changeup				
✕ Splitter				
▽ Slider	70.2%	83.8 [97]	5 [100]	-32.2 [103]
◇ Curveball				
⊕ Slow Curveball				
✳ Knuckleball				
▼ Screwball				

PLAYER COMMENTS WITHOUT GRAPHS

Akil Baddoo OF
Born: 08/16/98   Age: 21   Bats: L   Throws: L
Height: 6'1"   Weight: 210   Origin: Round 2, 2016 Draft (#74 overall)

YEAR	TEAM	LVL	AGE	PA	R	2B	3B	HR	RBI	BB	K	SB	CS	AVG/OBP/SLG
2017	TWI	RK	18	86	18	4	3	1	10	9	13	4	0	.267/.360/.440
2017	ELZ	RK	18	157	39	15	2	3	19	27	19	5	4	.357/.478/.579
2018	CDR	A	19	517	83	22	11	11	40	74	124	24	5	.243/.351/.419
2019	FTM	A+	20	131	15	3	3	4	9	12	39	6	2	.214/.290/.393
2020	MIN	MLB	21	251	24	12	2	6	26	22	80	4	1	.210/.284/.361

Comparables: Victor Robles, Jason Martin, Dilson Herrera

Baddoo cracked our organizational top-10 list last offseason, albeit with warning bells ringing. What began as an uneven full-season debut evolved into a reasonably strong second half in the Midwest League, but he gained some density and blanched at the sight of better breaking balls often enough to inspire concern for both his offensive and defensive skill sets. Sure enough Baddoo's whiff and walk rates wandered in the wrong directions during his tour of the Florida State League before late-May Tommy John surgery put the kibosh on any hopes for another second-half rebound. He'll bring a new elbow ligament with him on a return trip to Fort Myers this spring, with plenty of tools remaining but a long and uncertain path ahead.

YEAR	TEAM	LVL	AGE	PA	DRC+	VORP	BABIP	BRR	FRAA	WARP
2017	TWI	RK	18	86	143	4.9	.311	0.9	CF(8): -0.7	0.5
2017	ELZ	RK	18	157	194	27.1	.400	0.8	CF(28): -4.2	1.7
2018	CDR	A	19	517	117	30.7	.311	4.7	CF(97): -12.1, LF(3): 0.1	1.7
2019	FTM	A+	20	131	90	4.5	.280	1.6	CF(21): -2.7, LF(6): -0.2	0.1
2020	MIN	MLB	21	251	71	-1.2	.294	0.3	CF -4, LF 0	-0.6

Keoni Cavaco SS

Born: 06/02/01   Age: 19   Bats: R   Throws: R
Height: 6'2"   Weight: 195   Origin: Round 1, 2019 Draft (#13 overall)

YEAR	TEAM	LVL	AGE	PA	R	2B	3B	HR	RBI	BB	K	SB	CS	AVG/OBP/SLG
2019	TWI	RK	18	92	9	4	0	1	6	4	35	1	1	.172/.217/.253
2020	MIN	MLB	19	251	19	11	1	3	21	17	113	2	1	.194/.253/.291

Comparables: Billy Hamilton, Isan Díaz, Gavin Cecchini

Heading into the draft, scouts questioned how Cavaco would fare against steeper competition. The Twins, evidently unbothered by those qualms, selected him 13th overall—only to see him whiff 38 percent of the time in his first exposure to professional pitching. Ouch. Of course, there's no sense giving up on Cavaco. His struggles were expected to some degree, and he has the tools and athleticism to project as a potential middle-of-the-order hitter. We do think, however, that his development will entail moving to a non-shortstop position, thereby putting more pressure on his stick and greater emphasis on him figuring out pro-level stuff sooner than later.

YEAR	TEAM	LVL	AGE	PA	DRC+	VORP	BABIP	BRR	FRAA	WARP
2019	TWI	RK	18	92	28	-6.0	.275	-0.6	SS(20): 0.5	-0.3
2020	MIN	MLB	19	251	46	-9.7	.359	0.0	SS 0	-1.0

Gilberto Celestino OF

Born: 02/13/99 Age: 21 Bats: R Throws: L
Height: 6'0" Weight: 170 Origin: International Free Agent, 2015

YEAR	TEAM	LVL	AGE	PA	R	2B	3B	HR	RBI	BB	K	SB	CS	AVG/OBP/SLG
2017	GRV	RK	18	261	38	10	2	4	24	22	59	10	2	.268/.331/.379
2018	ELZ	RK	19	117	13	4	1	1	13	6	16	8	2	.266/.308/.349
2018	TCV	A-	19	142	18	8	0	4	21	10	25	14	0	.323/.387/.480
2019	CDR	A	20	503	52	24	3	10	51	48	81	14	8	.276/.350/.409
2019	FTM	A+	20	33	6	4	0	0	3	2	4	0	0	.300/.333/.433
2020	MIN	MLB	21	251	23	13	1	5	25	17	59	5	1	.233/.290/.361

Comparables: Brett Phillips, Dalton Pompey, Victor Robles

Another year, another steady step forward in the development of young Mr. Celestino. A tough first couple months melted into an encouraging full-season debut for the 20-year-old, who rode a smoother leg kick and weight transfer to more pop than expected in the Midwest League—all while flashing plenty of other above-average tools. His strong arm profiles well anywhere on the grass, while solid speed and instincts have kept a future in center firmly on the table. His timeline won't be confused with fellow July 2nd classmate Juan Soto's, but he remains on a nice track toward eventual everyday play in the big leagues.

YEAR	TEAM	LVL	AGE	PA	DRC+	VORP	BABIP	BRR	FRAA	WARP
2017	GRV	RK	18	261	102	14.1	.339	5.3	CF(43): 2.6, RF(8): 0.1	1.5
2018	ELZ	RK	19	117	89	-0.8	.301	1.1	CF(23): -1.0	0.2
2018	TCV	A-	19	142	175	15.2	.374	1.6	CF(16): 0.9, RF(12): 2.6	1.7
2019	CDR	A	20	503	137	22.7	.317	-3.6	CF(82): 3.7, RF(25): -3.6	3.0
2019	FTM	A+	20	33	124	3.5	.333	0.2	CF(4): -0.8, RF(3): -0.3	0.0
2020	MIN	MLB	21	251	74	-0.4	.292	0.0	CF 1, RF 0	0.1

Moises Gomez   OF
Born: 02/08/97   Age: 23   Bats: R   Throws: R
Height: 6'1"   Weight: 215   Origin: International Free Agent, 2015

When a scouting type describes someone as having "Large Richard" or "Willy Bobo" power, they're talking about the type of power that Gomez has. After a breakout at the dish in 2018 in the Midwest League, the slugger stalled a bit playing in the organization's home state. The hit tool has always been in question as he does not recognize spin all that well and can sell out for power. A sub-.230 average validates those concerns, but the good news is the power held up despite the large ballparks and more advanced arms—he finished the year among the Florida State League's top-10 in homers, doubles and total bases. No matter where his development goes from here, Gomez is a scouting success considering he signed for just $40,000 out of his native Venezuela in 2015.

Minnesota Twins 2020

Wander Javier SS
Born: 12/29/98   Age: 21   Bats: R   Throws: R
Height: 6'1"   Weight: 165   Origin: International Free Agent, 2015

YEAR	TEAM	LVL	AGE	PA	R	2B	3B	HR	RBI	BB	K	SB	CS	AVG/OBP/SLG
2017	ELZ	RK	18	180	34	13	1	4	22	19	49	4	3	.299/.383/.471
2019	CDR	A	20	342	43	9	1	11	37	35	116	2	0	.177/.278/.323
2020	MIN	MLB	21	251	20	11	1	5	23	18	98	1	0	.185/.252/.303

Comparables: Lane Thomas, Carter Kieboom, Oscar Hernández

For a couple of years there, Minnesota had paid $4 million so Dusty from Colorado could badger us on the internet. That changed last season, as Javier stayed healthy enough to log substantial playing time. That's the good news; the bad news is that he didn't play well. The rust on his barrel weighed it down and he struggled to catch up to velocity or connect with A-ball secondaries; there's still a long way for his body to go in terms of filling out as well. Javier looks like a stone-cold six-spotter on the dirt, and that's always a good place to start. But he has a long way to go before we feel comfortable pegging him as a big-league lock.

YEAR	TEAM	LVL	AGE	PA	DRC+	VORP	BABIP	BRR	FRAA	WARP
2017	ELZ	RK	18	180	127	17.2	.410	1.9	SS(36): -6.5	0.8
2019	CDR	A	20	342	70	2.1	.243	-0.9	SS(65): 2.0	0.3
2020	MIN	MLB	21	251	49	-8.9	.297	-0.3	SS 0	-0.9

Alex Kirilloff OF

Born: 11/09/97   Age: 22   Bats: L   Throws: L
Height: 6'2"   Weight: 195   Origin: Round 1, 2016 Draft (#15 overall)

YEAR	TEAM	LVL	AGE	PA	R	2B	3B	HR	RBI	BB	K	SB	CS	AVG/OBP/SLG
2018	CDR	A	20	281	36	20	5	13	56	24	47	1	1	.333/.391/.607
2018	FTM	A+	20	280	39	24	2	7	45	14	39	3	2	.362/.393/.550
2019	PEN	AA	21	411	47	18	2	9	43	29	76	7	6	.283/.343/.413
2020	MIN	MLB	22	251	26	14	1	8	31	14	58	0	0	.268/.315/.435

Comparables: Tyler Austin, Justin Williams, Gabriel Guerrero

The 15th pick in the 2016 draft, Kirilloff has experienced peaks and valleys throughout his pro career—accumulating displays of barrel work and injury issues alike. There's little doubt about his pure hitting ability, nor his size and strength; there's much doubt how the power translates, and whether enough will play to offset the penalties of a first-base-cum-corner-outfield defensive profile. Kirilloff didn't do a ton to answer those questions last year. That's not to take away from an impressive offensive effort as a 21-year-old in Double-A, nor is it to suggest he won't grow into a valuable player with the ability to anchor a lineup. He's capable of lifting his ceiling with a strong, healthy showing in the high minors this spring, and he could play his way firmly into the club's second-half plans.

YEAR	TEAM	LVL	AGE	PA	DRC+	VORP	BABIP	BRR	FRAA	WARP
2018	CDR	A	20	281	169	27.2	.364	-0.8	RF(53): -4.0, CF(1): 0.0	1.9
2018	FTM	A+	20	280	169	26.9	.399	-0.8	RF(51): 0.4, CF(3): 0.3	2.3
2019	PEN	AA	21	411	121	10.5	.333	-3.3	RF(41): -4.0, 1B(35): 0.3	0.6
2020	MIN	MLB	22	251	95	6.3	.325	-0.4	RF -3, 1B 0	0.4

Minnesota Twins 2020

Trevor Larnach OF
Born: 02/26/97 Age: 23 Bats: L Throws: R
Height: 6'4" Weight: 223 Origin: Round 1, 2018 Draft (#20 overall)

YEAR	TEAM	LVL	AGE	PA	R	2B	3B	HR	RBI	BB	K	SB	CS	AVG/OBP/SLG
2018	ELZ	RK	21	75	10	5	0	2	16	10	11	2	0	.311/.413/.492
2018	CDR	A	21	102	17	8	1	3	10	11	17	1	0	.297/.373/.505
2019	FTM	A+	22	361	33	26	1	6	44	35	74	4	1	.316/.382/.459
2019	PEN	AA	22	181	26	4	0	7	22	22	50	0	0	.295/.387/.455
2020	MIN	MLB	23	251	26	13	1	7	29	21	71	1	0	.258/.324/.409

Comparables: Zoilo Almonte, James Jones, Jordan Patterson

A year after signing underslot as the 20th-overall pick, Larnach was positively fine in his first full professional season. He split time between the Florida swamps, and in each place he hit the ball fine. The strikeout rate surged after his mid-season promotion to Double-A, but the game power started to play, so it was a fine trade-off. Scouts still see a defender who is entirely fine in either corner-outfield spot, too, as well a bat that should produce a bunch of dingers and an eye that should get him on base at an adequate rate. Franchise cornerstones are cool and all, but winning teams surround those types with ballplayers who can add value in various ways. Larnach appears that he's going to be fine in that role.

YEAR	TEAM	LVL	AGE	PA	DRC+	VORP	BABIP	BRR	FRAA	WARP
2018	ELZ	RK	21	75	157	5.5	.340	-1.5	RF(14): 3.8	0.8
2018	CDR	A	21	102	154	8.8	.338	0.7	RF(17): -1.5	0.7
2019	FTM	A+	22	361	165	22.2	.389	-1.4	RF(59): -8.1, LF(9): -0.4	1.9
2019	PEN	AA	22	181	146	13.9	.390	-0.3	RF(28): -2.2, LF(5): -0.1	0.8
2020	MIN	MLB	23	251	95	6.2	.344	-0.3	RF -4, LF 0	0.2

Royce Lewis SS

Born: 06/05/99 Age: 21 Bats: R Throws: R
Height: 6'2" Weight: 200 Origin: Round 1, 2017 Draft (#1 overall)

YEAR	TEAM	LVL	AGE	PA	R	2B	3B	HR	RBI	BB	K	SB	CS	AVG/OBP/SLG
2017	TWI	RK	18	159	38	6	2	3	17	19	17	15	2	.271/.390/.414
2017	CDR	A	18	80	16	2	1	1	10	6	16	3	1	.296/.363/.394
2018	CDR	A	19	327	50	23	0	9	53	24	49	22	4	.315/.368/.485
2018	FTM	A+	19	208	33	6	3	5	21	19	35	6	4	.255/.327/.399
2019	FTM	A+	20	418	55	17	3	10	35	27	90	16	8	.238/.289/.376
2019	PEN	AA	20	148	18	9	1	2	14	11	33	6	2	.231/.291/.358
2020	MIN	MLB	21	251	25	12	1	7	28	19	62	6	2	.231/.296/.383

Comparables: Cole Tucker, Alen Hanson, Jonathan Schoop

Lewis turned in possibly the most divisive season in all the minor-league land last season—or at least it seemed that way inside the BP Prospect Team's Slack channel. He continued to drop jaws with his explosiveness and elite physicality, as he's an 80-grade athlete who can show off in rapid bursts of coordinated, dynamic action. The baseball-specific movements, however, can still appear puzzlingly unrefined. For one thing, his quick-twitch start-up and plus foot speed haven't translated yet to acceptable success on stolen-base attempts. His agility is an asset at short, but the game clock and consistency remain in development and he saw reps just about everywhere else on the diamond in the AFL. And then there's the swing: a stiff, unathletic leg kick that'd get him banished from Radio City contributed to timing issues and below-average performance across two levels. His season was salvaged, to some extent, by an MVP campaign in fall ball. In spite of the litany of present warts, there's so much to get excited about with Lewis that we're sweet on his future.

YEAR	TEAM	LVL	AGE	PA	DRC+	VORP	BABIP	BRR	FRAA	WARP
2017	TWI	RK	18	159	159	18.1	.292	4.6	SS(32): -0.9	1.7
2017	CDR	A	18	80	111	6.5	.364	1.0	SS(17): 1.9	0.7
2018	CDR	A	19	327	156	31.3	.349	3.7	SS(67): 0.8	3.7
2018	FTM	A+	19	208	107	11.6	.291	1.7	SS(45): -4.8	0.7
2019	FTM	A+	20	418	97	15.0	.281	-1.5	SS(84): 4.0	1.8
2019	PEN	AA	20	148	67	7.8	.287	2.0	SS(28): -2.6, CF(1): 1.7	0.3
2020	MIN	MLB	21	251	81	2.1	.287	0.3	SS 0, CF 0	0.2

Minnesota Twins 2020

Brent Rooker OF

Born: 11/01/94   Age: 25   Bats: R   Throws: R
Height: 6'3"   Weight: 215   Origin: Round 1, 2017 Draft (#35 overall)

YEAR	TEAM	LVL	AGE	PA	R	2B	3B	HR	RBI	BB	K	SB	CS	AVG/OBP/SLG
2017	ELZ	RK	22	99	19	5	0	7	17	11	21	2	2	.282/.364/.588
2017	FTM	A+	22	162	23	6	0	11	35	16	47	0	0	.280/.364/.552
2018	CHT	AA	23	568	72	32	4	22	79	56	150	6	1	.254/.333/.465
2019	ROC	AAA	24	274	41	16	0	14	47	35	95	2	0	.281/.398/.535
2020	MIN	MLB	25	70	7	4	0	2	8	6	26	0	0	.218/.298/.389

Comparables: Chris Shaw, Joe Benson, Jake Lamb

Rooker likely would have debuted in the majors last season were it not for wrist and groin injuries. The story remains the same for the former 35th-overall pick: he'll need to mash, and he'll need to mash hard, if he's going to carve out a regular role at the highest level. Fortunately for him, he's now posted well above-average DRC+ numbers at every stop of his career, including last year's start-and-stop effort with the Triple-A moon ball. Rooker should get his first crack at the majors in 2020—he'll need to make the most of it, because his type is only a few hundred rough plate appearances from being tagged with the Quad-A label.

YEAR	TEAM	LVL	AGE	PA	DRC+	VORP	BABIP	BRR	FRAA	WARP
2017	ELZ	RK	22	99	134	10.3	.288	0.6	LF(17): 0.4	0.7
2017	FTM	A+	22	162	171	13.3	.341	-1.5	LF(16): -2.6, 1B(11): -0.4	0.8
2018	CHT	AA	23	568	117	13.2	.316	-4.7	1B(47): -5.7, LF(44): -8.2	0.0
2019	ROC	AAA	24	274	123	22.6	.417	2.6	LF(56): -0.6	1.5
2020	MIN	MLB	25	70	82	-0.5	.330	-0.1	LF -1	-0.1

Jorge Alcala   RHP
Born: 07/28/95   Age: 24   Bats: R   Throws: R
Height: 6'3"   Weight: 205   Origin: International Free Agent, 2014

YEAR	TEAM	LVL	AGE	W	L	SV	G	GS	IP	H	HR	BB/9	K/9	K	GB%	BABIP
2017	QUD	A	21	2	0	0	6	4	31	16	3	3.5	10.2	35	51%	.194
2017	BCA	A+	21	5	6	0	16	14	78^1	55	7	3.8	6.9	60	40%	.223
2018	BCA	A+	22	1	4	2	10	7	38^2	25	2	4.2	10.5	45	48%	.256
2018	CCH	AA	22	2	3	1	9	5	40^2	36	1	3.8	8.2	37	42%	.307
2018	CHT	AA	22	0	4	0	5	4	20	23	4	6.3	9.9	22	35%	.339
2019	PEN	AA	23	5	7	0	26	16	102^2	114	12	3.2	9.2	105	40%	.351
2019	ROC	AAA	23	1	0	0	5	0	7^2	4	0	2.3	12.9	11	60%	.267
2019	MIN	MLB	23	0	0	0	2	0	1^2	1	0	5.4	5.4	1	0%	.200
2020	MIN	MLB	24	3	3	0	27	5	48	47	8	5.2	7.5	40	38%	.285

Comparables: Hunter Wood, Robert Dugger, Brett Kennedy

We are all unique, but the human brain can't help but to order our natural world into patterns. No matter what anyone does, we all end up in buckets in other peoples' brains. There are worse baseball-related buckets than the "95-and-a-slider" one, even as it overflows. Alcala came one step closer to fulfilling that destiny in 2019, transitioning to the bullpen after his chuck-it command of four pitches torpedoed too many starts at Double-A. He promptly dominated in the role with a consolidated, short-burst arsenal that he rode all the way to the big-league debut that a lot of 95-and-a-slider prospects eventually enjoy. There's a little funk in his quick arm action, and therefore a little wiggle room with that loose command. If he can locate more consistently, he could land in Rocco Baldelli's "high-leverage" bucket sooner than later.

YEAR	TEAM	LVL	AGE	WHIP	ERA	DRA	WARP	MPH	FB%	WHF	CSP
2017	QUD	A	21	0.90	2.03	2.51	1.0				
2017	BCA	A+	21	1.12	3.45	3.70	1.4				
2018	BCA	A+	22	1.11	3.03	3.28	0.9				
2018	CCH	AA	22	1.30	3.54	3.91	0.6				
2018	CHT	AA	22	1.85	5.85	6.72	-0.3				
2019	PEN	AA	23	1.47	5.87	6.31	-1.8				
2019	ROC	AAA	23	0.78	0.00	1.89	0.3				
2019	MIN	MLB	23	1.20	0.00	5.77	0.0	97.0	65.5	17.2	36.6
2020	MIN	MLB	24	1.57	5.54	5.27	0.1	96.8	67.5	17.8	37.7

Jordan Balazovic RHP

Born: 09/17/98 Age: 21 Bats: R Throws: R
Height: 6'5" Weight: 215 Origin: Round 5, 2016 Draft (#153 overall)

YEAR	TEAM	LVL	AGE	W	L	SV	G	GS	IP	H	HR	BB/9	K/9	K	GB%	BABIP
2017	TWI	RK	18	1	3	0	10	3	40^1	47	5	4.5	6.5	29	37%	.331
2018	CDR	A	19	7	3	0	12	11	61^2	54	5	2.6	11.4	78	48%	.327
2019	CDR	A	20	2	1	0	4	4	20^2	15	1	1.7	14.4	33	42%	.318
2019	FTM	A+	20	6	4	0	15	14	73	52	3	2.6	11.8	96	45%	.283
2020	MIN	MLB	21	2	2	0	33	0	35	35	5	3.4	10.2	40	43%	.320

Comparables: German Márquez, Alex Reyes, Antonio Senzatela

A former fifth-rounder out of the relatively obscure Ontario prep ranks, Balazovic has blossomed into a big, highly projectable arm over the past couple years. He has an ideal frame with a steep release point, and he introduced himself to a lot of preference lists last year with dominant stretches of strikeout-heavy pitching across two levels of A-ball. There should be a couple more ticks to come as he continues filling out, which is an exciting proposition considering he's already advanced his secondaries. He should spend a good chunk of his age-21 season at Double-A, making him an arm to watch closely.

YEAR	TEAM	LVL	AGE	WHIP	ERA	DRA	WARP	MPH	FB%	WHF	CSP
2017	TWI	RK	18	1.66	4.91	8.77	-1.3				
2018	CDR	A	19	1.17	3.94	3.53	1.2				
2019	CDR	A	20	0.92	2.18	1.97	0.8				
2019	FTM	A+	20	1.00	2.84	3.23	1.6				
2020	MIN	MLB	21	1.38	4.77	4.70	0.2				

Matt Canterino   RHP

Born: 12/14/97   Age: 22   Bats: R   Throws: R
Height: 6'2"   Weight: 222   Origin: Round 2, 2019 Draft (#54 overall)

YEAR	TEAM	LVL	AGE	W	L	SV	G	GS	IP	H	HR	BB/9	K/9	K	GB%	BABIP
2019	CDR	A	21	1	1	0	5	5	20	6	0	3.2	11.2	25	49%	.146
2020	MIN	MLB	22	2	2	0	33	0	35	35	5	3.6	9.1	35	43%	.306

Comparables: Carl Edwards Jr., Michael Stutes, Jorge Alcala

The Twins saved a bit of money last June when they grabbed Canterino in the second round. A steady college performer at Rice, he signed for less than slot value to turn professional. Canterino then rode an above-average three-pitch mix to a stellar debut. The heater will tickle the mid-90s and features strong plane thanks to his higher arm slot, while both his bendy pitches receive solid reviews as potential bat-missers. He can(terino) dominate the low-minors, but don't be surprised if he can't(erino) succeed with similar aplomb against more mature hitters.

YEAR	TEAM	LVL	AGE	WHIP	ERA	DRA	WARP	MPH	FB%	WHF	CSP
2019	CDR	A	21	0.65	1.35	2.03	0.7				
2020	MIN	MLB	22	1.39	4.76	4.78	0.2				

Jhoan Duran   RHP

Born: 01/08/98   Age: 22   Bats: R   Throws: R
Height: 6'5"   Weight: 230   Origin: International Free Agent, 2014

YEAR	TEAM	LVL	AGE	W	L	SV	G	GS	IP	H	HR	BB/9	K/9	K	GB%	BABIP
2017	DIA	RK	19	0	2	0	3	3	11^1	19	0	3.2	10.3	13	64%	.452
2017	YAK	A-	19	6	3	0	11	11	51	44	5	3.0	6.4	36	54%	.253
2018	KNC	A	20	5	4	0	15	15	64^2	69	6	3.9	9.9	71	52%	.346
2018	CDR	A	20	2	1	0	6	6	36	19	2	2.5	11.0	44	66%	.218
2019	FTM	A+	21	2	9	0	16	15	78	63	5	3.6	11.0	95	53%	.317
2019	PEN	AA	21	3	3	0	7	7	37	34	2	2.2	10.0	41	64%	.349
2020	MIN	MLB	22	2	2	0	33	0	35	34	5	3.6	9.0	35	50%	.303

Comparables: Huascar Ynoa, Joel Payamps, Alex Cobb

The enormous Duran—listed at 6-foot-5 and 230 pounds—finally saw his stuff catch up to his frame last year. His lively four-seamer now touches triple digits, while a hammer curve darts down south of the zone off the same steep plane. If you caught him on the right day last season—like that May day when he whiffed 14 in just six innings, or his second-to-last start when he punched out 11 across eight scoreless—then you left thinking he sure looked like a front-of-the-rotation starter in the making. That might just be the case if he can progress further. Look for Duran to debut this summer.

YEAR	TEAM	LVL	AGE	WHIP	ERA	DRA	WARP	MPH	FB%	WHF	CSP
2017	DIA	RK	19	2.03	7.15	7.31	-0.1				
2017	YAK	A-	19	1.20	4.24	4.19	0.6				
2018	KNC	A	20	1.50	4.73	4.49	0.5				
2018	CDR	A	20	0.81	2.00	5.32	-0.1				
2019	FTM	A+	21	1.21	3.23	4.39	0.6				
2019	PEN	AA	21	1.16	4.86	6.27	-0.6				
2020	MIN	MLB	22	1.38	4.70	4.70	0.2				

Blayne Enlow   RHP

Born: 03/21/99   Age: 21   Bats: R   Throws: R
Height: 6'3"   Weight: 170   Origin: Round 3, 2017 Draft (#76 overall)

YEAR	TEAM	LVL	AGE	W	L	SV	G	GS	IP	H	HR	BB/9	K/9	K	GB%	BABIP
2017	TWI	RK	18	3	0	0	6	1	20^1	10	1	1.8	8.4	19	56%	.176
2018	CDR	A	19	3	5	1	20	17	94	94	4	3.4	6.8	71	47%	.315
2019	CDR	A	20	4	3	0	8	8	41^1	42	4	3.3	9.6	44	61%	.317
2019	FTM	A+	20	4	4	0	13	12	69^1	61	4	3.0	6.6	51	46%	.275
2020	MIN	MLB	21	2	2	0	33	0	35	34	5	3.5	6.1	24	46%	.272

Comparables: Jonathan Hernández, Nate Adcock, Mike Foltynewicz

Enlow stayed relatively healthy and grew quite a bit, both literally and in his approach on the mound. He added a bunch of the necessary strength and polish a highly-drafted prep arm invariably lacks, along with a hard slider to round out what is now a stout four-pitch mix. His fastball jumped into the mid-90s, as well, and while the results were mixed (as they often are for a still-filling-out 20-year-old pitching well above his age class), the foundation of a mid-rotation starter is now present. Health permitting, he should continue a rapid advance this year.

YEAR	TEAM	LVL	AGE	WHIP	ERA	DRA	WARP	MPH	FB%	WHF	CSP
2017	TWI	RK	18	0.69	1.33	1.16	1.0				
2018	CDR	A	19	1.37	3.26	5.10	0.1				
2019	CDR	A	20	1.38	4.57	4.72	0.2				
2019	FTM	A+	20	1.21	3.38	4.76	0.2				
2020	MIN	MLB	21	1.37	4.72	4.75	0.2				

Minnesota Twins 2020

Bailey Ober   RHP

Born: 07/12/95   Age: 24   Bats: R   Throws: R
Height: 6'9"   Weight: 260   Origin: Round 12, 2017 Draft (#346 overall)

YEAR	TEAM	LVL	AGE	W	L	SV	G	GS	IP	H	HR	BB/9	K/9	K	GB%	BABIP
2017	ELZ	RK	21	2	2	0	6	4	28	24	2	1.0	11.2	35	45%	.319
2018	CDR	A	22	7	1	0	14	14	75	71	7	1.1	10.6	88	44%	.337
2019	TWI	RK	23	1	0	0	2	1	9	6	0	1.0	13.0	13	71%	.286
2019	FTM	A+	23	4	0	0	8	8	45²	39	1	1.2	10.4	53	40%	.330
2019	PEN	AA	23	3	0	0	4	4	24	10	1	0.8	12.8	34	40%	.191
2020	MIN	MLB	24	2	2	0	33	0	35	35	5	2.9	10.2	40	40%	.318

Comparables: Brandon Workman, Cody Stashak, JD Hammer

Any time a pitcher yields all of six earned runs across an entire season—one spanning nearly 80 innings and three minor-league levels—it's bound to catch an inquisitive eye or three. And when the pitcher doing it stands 6-foot-9? Interest tends to grow to a similar scale from there. Not so with Ober, as the scouting community remains unimpressed. He uses every inch of his extra-large frame to generate outrageous downhill plane with an over-the-top delivery, and it helps a good changeup perform great against minor-league hitters. Unfortunately, his fastball tops out around 87 mph, and there's only so far that tends to take a pitcher in this day and age. Nevertheless, he should get his chance to prove the critics wrong this season, and stranger things have happened than an unorthodox 12th-round reliever figuring out how to pull rabbits out of his hat.

YEAR	TEAM	LVL	AGE	WHIP	ERA	DRA	WARP	MPH	FB%	WHF	CSP
2017	ELZ	RK	21	0.96	3.21	2.09	1.2				
2018	CDR	A	22	1.07	3.84	3.39	1.6				
2019	TWI	RK	23	0.78	0.00	0.92	0.5				
2019	FTM	A+	23	0.99	0.99	3.38	0.9				
2019	PEN	AA	23	0.50	0.38	2.00	0.9				
2020	MIN	MLB	24	1.30	4.30	4.36	0.3				

LINEOUTS

Hitters

HITTER	POS	TEAM	LVL	AGE	PA	R	2B	3B	HR	RBI	BB	K	SB	CS	AVG/OBP/SLG	DRC+	WARP
Travis Blankenhorn	UT	PEN	AA	22	410	50	18	2	18	51	18	93	11	0	.278/.312/.474	119	2.5
	UT	FTM	A+	22	61	6	4	0	1	3	9	12	0	0	.269/.377/.404	133	0.2
Nick Gordon	MI	ROC	AAA	23	319	49	29	3	4	40	18	65	14	4	.298/.342/.459	107	1.5
Seth Gray	3B	ELZ	Rk+	21	257	34	15	0	11	36	30	53	4	1	.225/.336/.445	112	1.3
Will Holland	SS	ELZ	Rk+	21	145	22	2	0	7	16	14	44	8	1	.192/.299/.376	72	0.3
Ryan Jeffers	C	PEN	AA	22	99	13	5	0	4	9	9	19	0	0	.287/.374/.483	142	0.8
	C	FTM	A+	22	315	35	11	0	10	40	28	64	0	0	.256/.330/.402	122	1.6
Ryan LaMarre	OF	GWN	AAA	30	455	55	24	8	9	53	38	118	19	9	.311/.380/.477	112	2.4
	OF	MIN	MLB	30	26	3	0	0	2	3	3	5	1	1	.217/.308/.478	97	0.0
Gabriel Maciel	OF	CDR	A	20	187	28	3	4	0	17	23	31	8	2	.309/.395/.377	135	1.2
	OF	FTM	A+	20	229	29	6	2	3	17	21	30	14	7	.261/.342/.357	117	1.2
Jose Miranda	INF	FTM	A+	21	478	48	25	1	8	55	24	54	0	0	.248/.299/.364	103	1.3
Luke Raley	OF	ROC	AAA	24	138	28	6	0	7	21	7	42	4	0	.302/.362/.516	118	0.9
Yunior Severino	INF	CDR	A	19	86	7	7	0	0	8	7	27	0	0	.244/.302/.333	95	0.1
Spencer Steer	INF	ELZ	Rk+	21	95	14	6	1	2	13	15	5	0	1	.325/.442/.506	165	1.0
	INF	CDR	A	21	201	26	12	2	2	20	19	28	5	1	.260/.358/.387	129	0.8
LaMonte Wade Jr	LF	MIN	MLB	25	69	10	2	1	2	5	11	9	0	1	.196/.348/.375	105	0.2
	LF	ROC	AAA	25	334	47	12	1	5	24	56	48	7	2	.246/.392/.356	106	0.3
Matt Wallner	OF	CDR	A	21	53	7	3	1	2	6	5	14	0	0	.205/.340/.455	114	-0.1
	OF	ELZ	Rk+	21	238	35	18	1	6	28	19	66	1	1	.269/.361/.452	133	1.2
Zander Wiel	1B	ROC	AAA	26	522	86	40	5	24	78	40	158	2	1	.254/.320/.514	101	1.3

Not to be confused with a slow-footed mountain goat, **Travis Blankenhorn** is a slow-seasoning prospect whose inconsistencies of approach and leather have left the former third-rounder staring up a rocky slope to the majors. ⓧ **Nick Gordon** held his own when healthy at Triple-A last year, but these days he looks more like a depth-chart puzzle piece than a regular. ⓧ A good glove and plenty of pop got **Seth Gray** drafted in the fourth round. His bat will need to find some color if it's going to play at the highest levels ⓧ The Twins paid third-round money in the fifth for **Will Holland** and all they got was this crappy t-shirt and a 30-percent whiff rate in short-season ball. ⓧ **Ryan Jeffers** impressed on both sides in his first full pro season, showing power potential at the plate and making strides with his receiving behind it. After a successful cameo at Double-A, he looks to be the rare fast-moving catching prospect. Should everything go well, he might elbow his way onto the big-league depth chart at some point this season. ⓧ The Twins brought back **Ryan LaMarre** to fill some September at-bats, clearing the way for him to log big-league playing time for the fifth consecutive season. He'll look to keep that streak alive in 2020 despite being short on tools—and on time left in his prime. ⚾ So far, so good for **Gabriel Maciel**, a 20-year-old speed-and-leather prospect whose bat held serve after a midseason promotion to High-A. ⚾ A former second-rounder, **Jose Miranda** hung in there against Florida State League pitching. His stick will have to show it can do more than that after he shed his shortstop ambitions. ⚾ Ugly approach notwithstanding, **Luke Raley** raked at Triple-A before breaking his ankle in May. He has large muscles and some versatility, and he should be in the mix for big-league at-bats in 2020. ⚾ A casualty of the Braves' international signing scandal a couple years back, **Yunior Severino** resurfaced with Minnesota and appeared poised to take a leap in full-season ball last year before a broken thumb derailed him for two and a half months. He has some pop but a raw approach and hazy defensive future. ⚾ The club's third-rounder last June, **Spencer Steer** is a high-floor utility prospect with a solid hit tool and excellent defensive skills. The Twins will try to herd him up to Minnesota on a quicker timeline after his successful pro debut. ⚾ The centerpiece of Minnesota's 2018 international spending strategy, **Misael Urbina** looked great out of the gate in his Dominican debut and should see the American seashore this season. ⚾ **LaMonte Wade, Jr.** gets on base a lot, and the skill held after about 18 injuries cleared a path for him to big-league at-bats down the stretch. He'll need to find another defining trait (or three) if he's going to garner more playing time in 2020. ⚾ The 39th overall pick last June, **Matt Wallner** is a big boy with big-boy power, big-boy length to his swing, and a big-boy fastball in his back pocket in case the second thing torpedoes the first thing. ⚾ After spending decades as a famous Coney Island landmark **Zander Wiel** will shift gears and try his hand at supplanting C.J. Cron as a cheaper block of corner-masher wood for the Twins' fire.

Pitchers

PITCHER	TEAM	LVL	AGE	W	L	SV	G	GS	IP	H	HR	BB/9	K/9	K	GB%	WHIP	ERA	DRA	WARP
Dakota Chalmers	TWI	Rk	22	1	0	0	4	4	13^1	8	0	5.4	12.8	19	68%	1.20	4.05	2.34	0.5
	FTM	A+	22	1	1	0	5	5	21^1	12	0	6.3	12.2	29	55%	1.27	3.38	3.49	0.4
Trevor Hildenberger	ROC	AAA	28	1	0	2	14	0	19	19	2	1.9	7.1	15	46%	1.21	4.74	3.75	0.5
	MIN	MLB	28	2	2	1	22	0	16^1	30	2	3.9	8.3	15	41%	2.27	10.47	7.51	-0.4
Griffin Jax	PEN	AA	24	4	5	0	20	20	111^1	98	5	1.9	6.8	84	50%	1.10	2.67	4.32	0.9
	ROC	AAA	24	1	2	0	3	3	16	19	2	1.7	5.6	10	46%	1.38	4.50	5.60	0.2
Ryan O'Rourke	ROC	AAA	31	2	1	0	7	0	12	7	0	9.0	10.5	14	39%	1.58	4.50	5.63	0.1
	SYR	AAA	31	2	3	2	36	2	44	39	4	4.7	9.6	47	53%	1.41	3.27	4.31	0.8
	NYN	MLB	31	0	0	0	2	0	1^1	0	0	20.2	6.8	1	0%	2.25	0.00	8.30	0.0
Sean Poppen	PEN	AA	25	2	3	0	8	7	28^2	30	0	5.3	12.2	39	59%	1.64	4.40	5.73	-0.3
	ROC	AAA	25	5	1	0	12	9	61	53	4	4.0	10.0	68	58%	1.31	3.84	3.69	1.7
	MIN	MLB	25	0	0	0	4	0	8^1	10	1	5.4	9.7	9	46%	1.80	7.56	5.83	0.0
Chris Vallimont	CLN	A	22	4	4	0	13	13	69^1	48	4	3.4	10.4	80	41%	1.07	2.99	3.10	1.7
	JUP	A+	22	2	3	0	6	6	36	31	3	2.8	10.5	42	30%	1.17	3.50	4.71	0.1
	FTM	A+	22	2	2	0	4	4	22^1	15	0	1.6	11.3	28	38%	0.85	3.63	5.47	-0.1

Oakland popped **Dakota Chalmers** in the third round in 2015. Then he couldn't throw strikes; then he popped his UCL; then he got shipped to the midwest; and now he's back to not throwing strikes. His misses can touch 97 mph and buckle knees, however. ⓥ **Trevor Hildenberger** was just okay at Triple-A before a catastrophic late-season return to the Show sealed his non-tender fate with the Twins. He'll look to recapture glory on someone else's Triple-A roster this year. ⓥ A former third-rounder, **Griffin Jax** has been fakin' his way through Double-A, leaning on good command of moving stuff to stymie Southern League hitters despite a concerning lack of whiffs. He'll be in the mix for rotation innings in the year ahead. ⓥ Dual Irish/American citizen **Ryan O'Rourke** went over to Bulgaria and closed a couple games for the Irish national team in the European Baseball Championships during a week of DFA limbo in the middle of last summer. ⓥ **Sean Poppen's** elbow didn't go full onomatopoeia, but it did bark loud enough to knock him out for the season a mere four games into his big-league career. It was an unfortunate injury, but his Engineering Sciences degree from Harvard should come in handy should his wing ever require structural reconfiguration. ⓥ A sneaky late-season grab for Sergio Romo's services, **Chris Vallimont** brings a legendary D-II pedigree and serious strikeout potential. He's not as good of a prospect as his numbers suggest, but he's one worth keeping tabs on.

Twins Prospects

The State of the System

The Twins system is deep enough now that I got legitimately annoyed I couldn't get a few of my favorite names on here.

The Top Ten

─────── ★ ★ ★ *2020 Top 101 Prospect* **#21** ★ ★ ★ ───────

1 **Royce Lewis** **SS**   OFP: 70   ETA: 2020/21
Born: 06/05/99 Age: 21 Bats: R Throws: R Height: 6'2" Weight: 200
Origin: Round 1, 2017 Draft (#1 overall)

The Report: Don't scout the stat line is one of the older adages in prospect writing. It's generally good advice. But performance always needs to be explained, good or bad. Sometimes it's obvious, matching up to the tools and projection, like when Vlad Jr. hits .400 for a few months, or Ronald Acuña torches three levels of the minors. Sometimes there's an easy explanation for a mismatch of production and projection—a college arm spamming a fringy slider in the Appy League to video game K-rates, a teenaged bat struggling in cold Midwest League parks, a polished college slugger coming off a broken hamate.

Royce Lewis did not hit like a Top 10 national prospect this year. And yes, there's an explanation.

Lewis played another three-plus months of games—including a promotion to Double-A and an MVP Fall League campaign—since Keanan's piece detailing his swing issues. I saw the same issues at Futures, a needlessly long hand path, upper and lower halves constantly out of sync. I also saw premium hand speed once the bat starts moving forward, and top-of-the-scale athleticism. Ricky saw the same issues in Arizona, but his love of the athletic tools and the potential of the offensive profile won out.

I point all this out in a rather long preamble because Lewis might be the single most divisive prospect internally at BP, but we also all broadly agree on the All-Star OFP. Lewis has a chance to be a true five-tool player with 55s or better everywhere while playing a premium defensive position, perhaps a couple of them. But the difficulty level only ratchets up from here, and if the swing problems remain, Lewis could be putting up similarly puzzling stat lines in the majors. It should all work out. He has premium bat speed and body control, game-changing speed, plus raw power, defensive flexibility.

STEPHEN A: BUT!

Variance: High. Man, I'd almost be tempted to go extreme, which is a OFP/Variance combo I would normally only consider for generational IFA signees or post-TJ Lucas Giolito types. The athleticism is so good, Lewis can carve out a major league career even if the swing remains an endless work in progress. If he does sort things out...well, the OFP won't be light per se, but it might be a lot of all-star games.

Mark Barry's Fantasy Take: One might think that posting an OPS below .700 across two levels would create a buy-low opportunity for a top prospect. The fact that Lewis's stock hasn't really dropped all that much is a good indicator of how highly he's valued in the community. He's still a top 10-15 dynasty prospect, although the risk factor might be slightly higher than where it was this time last year.

★ ★ ★ *2020 Top 101 Prospect* **#32** ★ ★ ★

2 Brusdar Graterol   RHP   OFP: 70   ETA: 2019
Born: 08/26/98   Age: 21   Bats: R   Throws: R   Height: 6'1"   Weight: 265
Origin: International Free Agent, 2014

The Report: Graterol got off to a dominant start in the Pensacola rotation before going down with an shoulder impingement. He came back two months later and the Twins moved him to the bullpen for the rest of his season, which included a September cup of coffee with the big club. In the pen he showed an 80-grade sinker that routinely hit triple-digits and featured patently unfair movement. There's a slider that he ramps up into the low-90s and is a potential plus-plus offering as well. It's one of the best two-pitch combos you will find among prospect arms, and there's only a handful of major league arms that can boast something better.

So there's going to be a strong temptation to keep Braterol in the bullpen. 2019 only added to a bad injury track record that already includes a Tommy John surgery. However, Graterol is only 21, and he has shown feel for a potentially average change—although one of the three he threw in the majors per Brooks resulted in a very long Zack Collins home run. He's not quite as max effort with the delivery as a starter, but it's not exactly Greg Maddux either. The Twins have rotation spots to offer in 2020, and I'd be tempted to at least give him a shot firing bullets every fifth day. The upside could be worth it, and hey, that elite reliever fallback isn't going anywhere.

Variance: High. The durability track record isn't good and the reliever risk is significant.

Mark Barry's Fantasy Take: As a once silent-cowboy-turned-old-guy-yelling-at-an-empty-chair man once said, "You've got to ask yourself one question: Do I feel lucky?" The range of outcomes is huge with Graterol, and the most likely scenario isn't the most fun for fantasy purposes. Still, his ceiling is so high and the floor (non-injury version) is a very good closer, so he'll stay in the top-60 or so fairly easily.

--- ★ ★ ★ *2020 Top 101 Prospect* **#85** ★ ★ ★ ---

3. Trevor Larnach   OF   OFP: 55   ETA: 2020/21
Born: 02/26/97   Age: 23   Bats: L   Throws: R   Height: 6'4"   Weight: 223
Origin: Round 1, 2018 Draft (#20 overall)

The Report: Larnach and Kirilofff are a matched pair in my mind, but that's harder to convey visually with all the biographic info on the top half of these lists. Both are polished corner bats that haven't hit for quite as much game power or quite as much in general as you might like given the defensive limitations in the profiles. Larnach was a college pick, Kiriloff a prep bat, but he's only nine months older and both ended the year in Double-A. So at this point it's a fairly dead rubber on age-relative-to-league.

Larnach has plus raw power and enough uppercut to his swing where you'd think it'd get into games more, but he struggles to consistently lift the ball as often as your typical prospect sluggers. He already makes a lot of hard line drive contact so it shouldn't take much of a tweak to turn some of those doubles into home runs, and he's strong enough to drive the ball to all fields. But it hasn't happened yet. Larnach can get passive and struggle with offspeed, but there's enough bat speed and he'll do enough damage on fastballs to project at least an average hit tool. That should allow the raw power to play enough to carry an otherwise nondescript corner outfield profile.

Variance: Medium. He's a high college pick that has performed well enough at every stop, but the defensive and athletic limitations means that will have to continue.

Mark Barry's Fantasy Take: Getting serious Nicholas Castellanos vibes (or like, prime Kole Calhoun) from Larnach, as he could be a guy that doesn't play much defense but launches maybe 25-30 homers and hits for a decent average. It's probably a better profile for fantasy than in real life, but luckily that's all we care about in this here blurb.

--- ★ ★ ★ *2020 Top 101 Prospect* **#86** ★ ★ ★ ---

4. Alex Kirilloff   OF   OFP: 55   ETA: 2020/21
Born: 11/09/97   Age: 22   Bats: L   Throws: L   Height: 6'2"   Weight: 195
Origin: Round 1, 2016 Draft (#15 overall)

The Report: While Larnach's prospect profile has been slow and steady, a late first round college pick who climbs prospect rankings bit by bit as he hits at every stop, Kiriloff's has been a bit more of a yo-yo. He announced himself quickly after the draft, mashing in the Appy League and garnering better reports on the bat than you'd expect from a cold weather prep without much athletic projection.

Tommy John surgery then cost him all of 2017, injecting a fair bit of uncertainty into the profile. 2018 came and he destroyed two A-ball levels, although the performance outpaced the tools and it started to look more likely he'd slide from a corner outfield spot to first base. 2019 was uneven at the plate, although you could easily point out that he was 21 in Double-A and missed the first month with a wrist injury. Those tend to linger. But he made some swing changes that geared him more for pull power and affected his plate coverage and ability to hit to all fields. He also played almost as much first base as outfield, and the cold corner may be his long term home. On the other hand, he did heat up and hit for more power towards the end of the year.

In conclusion, Alex Kiriloff is a land of contrasts.

He also remains a good prospect and not that far off from the potential plus hit/power guy you're still expecting.

Variance: Medium. If he slides to first base, that means he will really have to hit. The injuries can explain away the early season production issues, but he's also had a fair bit of injuries now, and they are of the type that can sap offensive skills.

Mark Barry's Fantasy Take: I'm targeting Kiriloff wherever I can. Sure, more injuries are troubling, but now is the time to pounce, especially since his shift to the cold corner likely means an expedited path to the big leagues. Despite the scrapes and bruises, Kiriloff still maintained above-average contact and even chipped in a handful of steals. He's still firmly in the top-15ish for me as far as dynasty prospects are concerned.

5. Jhoan Duran RHP

OFP: 60   ETA: 2020/21
Born: 01/08/98   Age: 22   Bats: R   Throws: R   Height: 6'5"   Weight: 230
Origin: International Free Agent, 2014

The Report: If you liked Brusdar Graterol, you'll like Jhoan Duran. It's the same type of power stuff. Duran can work his high-spin, four-seam fastball up over 100 and he complements it with a diving, mid-90s sinker/splitter hybrid. He also throws a power 11-5 breaker that he can run up into the upper-80s and will flash plus-plus. It's an ideal starter's fame, but not ideal starter's mechanics due to some late effort that causes him to fall off to the first base side. So it's not exactly easy velocity, and his command and control play on the fringe side of average.

If you think the second fastball look is enough of a change of pace, you could already give Duran credit for three plus major league pitches. Honestly even if you don't buy that taxonomy, the different fastball looks combined with the breaking ball might be enough to start anyway, but given the mechanics, and what he might be able to offer in short bursts, like with Graterol the temptation to unleash him at the end of games might be too great.

Variance: High. Limited upper minors experience, high relief risk.

Mark Barry's Fantasy Take: So, I'm not as high on Duran for fantasy, moreso because of the delivery as opposed to the arsenal. Even if he starts, it's hard to pencil him in as a guy that wades into the sixth and seventh innings with consistency. Like Graterol, Duran could be a lights out reliever, but that dramatically decreases his fantasy upside.

6. Keoni Cavaco   SS   OFP: 55   ETA: 2023
Born: 06/02/01   Age: 19   Bats: R   Throws: R   Height: 6'2"   Weight: 195
Origin: Round 1, 2019 Draft (#13 overall)

The Report: The Twins moved Cavaco from third base to shortstop full time after drafting him—he played a bit of both in high school and on the showcase circuit—and he certainly looks the part of a highly-touted SoCal prep shortstop. He has a left side arm and is a plus runner. If he does have to slide back to third as he enters his twenties and fills out, the quick twitch athleticism should make him comfortably above-average there. He has enough raw power for a corner spot too, although the swing can be a little stiff in the upper half at times to generate the pop. Cavaco was a pop-up name that only turned 18 right before draft day, so he is going to take some time to develop as a professional, but the speed/power combo will be intriguing wherever he ends up the diamond.

Variance: Very high. Complex-league resume, shorter amateur track record, hit tool questions. If he does stick at short and the bat comes good, however, Cavaco has the potential to make a few all-star games.

Mark Barry's Fantasy Take:

7. Jordan Balazovic   RHP   OFP: 55   ETA: 2021
Born: 09/17/98   Age: 21   Bats: R   Throws: R   Height: 6'5"   Weight: 215
Origin: Round 5, 2016 Draft (#153 overall)

The Report: Playing the entire season at 20, Balazovic blitzed two A-ball levels on the strength of his mid-90s fastball, which shows life up and sink down. He has two potentially average major league secondaries as well. The best of the two at present is a mid-80s slider that he can manipulate to spot in the zone, or to induce swings out of it. The latter version is preferable, firmer with good tilt. The changeup is more of a projection pitch at present, but he maintains his arm speed well, and it will flash average fade. The slider needs more consistent shape, the change more consistent location, but they should end up quality offerings to play off the plus fastball.

Balazovic has a good frame and while his uptempo delivery can occasionally get out of sync, he generally repeats his mechanics well. If he continues to refine his secondaries, he should be ready to step into the middle of the Twins rotation in a year or two.

Variance: Medium. Secondaries need further development, and he hasn't seen Double-A yet. If you believe the conventional wisdom that cold weather prep arms can pop later, well, Canada is pretty cold.

Mark Barry's Fantasy Take: I like Balazovic quite a bit more than Duran and Cavaco for fantasy, as he's a huge dude that could shoulder a relatively-full starter's workload. Also appealing: he punched out around a third of the guys he faced last season. Pair those two things together and you have a guy who could bust out of the dreaded "mid-rotation-starter" mold.

8   Lewis Thorpe   LHP

OFP: 55   ETA: 2019
Born: 11/23/95   Age: 24   Bats: R   Throws: L   Height: 6'1"   Weight: 218
Origin: International Free Agent, 2012

The Report: It feels like we have been writing about Thorpe forever, but despite that—and despite missing two full seasons due to Tommy John—he only just turned 24. He's also made the majors now, and while the best hitters in the world weren't particularly kind to him during his debut, the stuff remains major-league-quality, if not particularly superlative.

Thorpe is a four-pitch lefty that likes to mix his full arsenal. The fastball is mostly low-90s and a little true—although he will occasionally cut it in to righties—but there's deception from his delivery, and the pitch can be effective when he spots it around the edges of the zone. The slider was his primary secondary in the majors and it's developed into a potential swing-and-miss offering in the mid-80s despite showing more cutterish action than two-plane break. The changeup got punished badly in the majors, and he hung too many of them, but it's had average action and projection in the past. There's a mid-70s lollipop curve for a different breaking ball look to round things out. Thorpe's command simply wasn't fine enough during his major league debut, but he continued to miss bats like he always has. If he can consistently get ahead of major league hitters and keep his stuff out of the middle of the zone, there's the potential for an above-average major league starter, but the likely outcome here is more of a backend guy that's a little too hittable.

Variance: Medium. Thorpe made the majors and at time of publication his main competition for an Opening Day 2020 rotation spot are Devin Smeltzer and Randy Dobnak. There's some downside risk here if the stuff just can't consistently get outs, but he's a lefty with a broad arsenal, he'll likely find a major league role of some sort.

Mark Barry's Fantasy Take: Thorpe is moderately more interesting if you're in the middle of your deep-league contention cycle, as he could help your rotation as early as this year. I don't know if there's much more than a fantasy SP4 on the high end, but he should tally a bunch of strikeouts, if underwhelming elsewhere.

9. Ryan Jeffers   C
OFP: 55   **ETA:** 2021
Born: 06/03/97   Age: 23   Bats: R   Throws: R   Height: 6'4"   Weight: 230
Origin: Round 2, 2018 Draft (#59 overall)

The Report: Jeffers made it to Double-A by the end of his first full professional season, that's moving pretty quickly for a second-round college catcher. The bat has really yet to be challenged by professional pitching and the power has continued to develop in games, which has paved his speedy path up the organizational ladder. There's a potential 50/55 hit/power combination here, and Jeffers has filled out his lean frame and improved his receiving. He has an above-average arm as well, so there's true two-way catcher upside in the profile now. If you want to find a potential breakout Top 101 name in the Twins system for next year, look no further.

Variance: High. Catchers are weird. Jeffers still has some strides to make defensively and the bat might be ready for the majors before the glove is.

Mark Barry's Fantasy Take: A bat-first catcher, you say? You have my attention. If you have roster space, and can stomach rolling the dice on a fantasy catcher, Jeffers is as good an under-the-radar name as any. There's risk he might have to move to first base, in which case he's less interesting, but Jeffers is an easy name for a flier in deep leagues.

10. Gilberto Celestino   OF
OFP: 55   **ETA:** 2021/22
Born: 02/13/99   Age: 21   Bats: R   Throws: L   Height: 6'0"   Weight: 170
Origin: International Free Agent, 2015

The Report: Celestino sticks in the number ten spot again this year, but that obscures some improvements in the profile. He's gotten a little more comfortable lifting the ball pull side, so while the approach remains mostly gap-to-gap, he could sneak 10-15 bombs over the left field fence as well. He's also added some good weight in his lower half which has stabilized the leg kick in his swing and given everything a bit more oomph offensively. Last year, we were still questioning how much Celestino would hit, and while a season in A-ball won't answer all concerns, we're more confident now in at least average hit tool here.

The center field profile remains no-doubt. He's an above-average runner whose speed plays up on the grass because of his excellent instincts. He picks out the landing spot, and then goes and gets it, rarely drifting to the ball. The defense remains the carrying tool, but the improving bat makes it more likely Celestino gets penciled into the lineup every day.

Variance: High. There's still a limited professional track record with the bat.

Mark Barry's Fantasy Take: Bret suggested Ender Inciarte as a nonzero outcome for Celestino, and with the improvements in his game, namely hitting for contact and stealing some bases, that still feels kinda right. It might not be sexy (or necessary to run out and roster him), but Inciarte was good for a bit, right?

Minnesota Twins 2020

The Next Ten

11   Devin Smeltzer   LHP
Born: 09/07/95   Age: 24   Bats: R   Throws: L   Height: 6'3"   Weight: 195
Origin: Round 5, 2016 Draft (#161 overall)

It's not a secret I'm a sucker for a lefty sitting in the upper-80s with a good changeup, but usually those pitchers end up in the "Personal Cheeseball" section below. Bonus points if they have rec-specs and a questionable goatee. Smeltzer checks all those boxes, but his change has developed into a swing-and-miss pitch against righties at the highest level, with plus fade and sink and a deceptive arm action more than making up for less than ideal separation off the fastball. A mid-70s, big breaking, 1-7 curve is similarly deployed against lefties, an his low-three-quarters slot makes it look like the breaker starts at their ear flap.

Smeltzer will throw one of the above-average offspeeds about half the time, which makes sense given that the fastball merely touches 90. He's confident enough to throw it to either side of the plate, and he can sneak it by you if you are focused on the secondaries. It's a profile with thin margins, but Meltzer's arsenal and approach have yet to wobble against big league bats, and while there's not a ton of upside, he looks like a fairly safe backend starter or swingman. Minnesota's lineup might be mashing home runs by the bunches now, but it's nice to see that they still employ at least one extremely Twins Pitcher™.

12   Nick Gordon   IF
Born: 10/24/95   Age: 24   Bats: L   Throws: R   Height: 6'0"   Weight: 160
Origin: Round 1, 2014 Draft (#5 overall)

In the beginning God created the heaven and the earth. Then he wrote up a Nick Gordon prospect blurb. When I wrote above that "[i]t feels like we have been writing about Thorpe forever," that's not nearly as long as we've been writing about Gordon, whose high school scouting report was the second thing to come off Gutenberg's press. Jokes aside, he's still just 24, and hit in Triple-A in a repeat engagement truncated at the front by acute gastritis and at the back by a leg bruise. Gordon is unlikely to hit the heights implied when drafted fifth overall as a prep shortstop, but he's come back around to perhaps being a bit underrated. He is high-waisted and athletic with a loose, contact-oriented swing, but he's never really developed much physicality and it's a smallish frame. There is sneaky doubles pop, and he's a pesky at-bat, but aggressive enough that walks aren't going to be a huge part of his game. There's an above-average hit tool here on balance, and Gordon can handle either middle infield spot. He's a better fit at second, so there's some Joe Panik in the profile, but Panik was a decent starter for a few years. It's not a smash hit from a top-five pick, but it's a pretty good prospect to have outside your top ten.

13 **Brent Rooker   OF/1B**
Born: 11/01/94   Age: 25   Bats: R   Throws: R   Height: 6'3"   Weight: 215
Origin: Round 1, 2017 Draft (#35 overall)

I wonder if Rooker feels a bit left out from the Twins offensive explosion in 2019. He's a perfect fit for the parade of bash brothers that rolled out in Target Field. Rooker was heating up and putting himself in contention for a MLB call up when a groin injury functionally ended his season in mid-July. He's an ideal hitter for our rabbit ball/launch angle era, and while strikeouts continue (and likely will continue) to be an issue there's enough pop and approach to get him above the Quad-A line and into the middle of a major league lineup for a few years. He's limited to left field, first base and designated hitter, all areas the Twins have plenty of MLB options, so it might take someone else's injury misfortune to open a spot for Rooker.

14 **Matt Wallner   OF**
Born: 12/12/97   Age: 22   Bats: L   Throws: R   Height: 6'5"   Weight: 220
Origin: Round 1, 2019 Draft (#39 overall)

The Twins do like their corner guys with pop, and they added another one to the org with their Comp A pick. They might have gotten the biggest raw in the draft class, and Wallner gets there without a huge load or all that much length to the swing. He does like to get extended, and struggles to adjust his bat path once he commits so he could struggle with velocity inside or adjusting to breaking stuff. He'll be fine enough in right field, as he's athletic for his size and was up to 97 in college when he was still pitching. The present issues hit tool will likely limit how much the prodigious power plays, but the native Minnesotan has pop enough to spare.

15 **Cole Sands   RHP**
Born: 07/17/97   Age: 22   Bats: R   Throws: R   Height: 6'3"   Weight: 215
Origin: Round 5, 2018 Draft (#154 overall)

In his feature on gaming the draft, former BP Prospect staff member and current Pirates Quantitative Analyst, Grant Jones suggested Cole Sands as one of the prep prospects to target as a significantly overslot pick in later rounds. Sands ended up going to Florida State and was drafted in the fifth round in 2018 after an uneven college career. Grant was onto something though, as Sands pitched at three levels in 2019, finding success working off a fastball that he can dial up to 95 with late run. There's an average curve—that flashes higher when it shows true 12-6 action— and potentially average change-up. Sands has pretty much the ideal starting pitcher body, but the delivery is a bit upright and arm-heavy. He's yet to throw 100 innings in a season, but once that hurdle is cleared, the profile looks like a solid number four starter.

16 — Misael Urbina   OF
Born: 04/26/02   Age: 18   Bats: R   Throws: R   Height: 6'0"   Weight: 175
Origin: International Free Agent, 2018

One of the top prospects in the 2018 IFA class, Urbina is more polish than tools with an advanced approach and hit tool for a 17-year-old. The swing would look good at any age, balanced and able to drive the ball from line to line. He's far from a finished product, and could add 20 pounds or so without impacting his above-average speed and center field glove projection. How much power Urbina ultimately develops will determine if we are looking at a plus regular or more of a cromulent everyday guy, but he's advanced enough at present to handle a fairly aggressive stateside assignment in 2020 if the Twins were so inclined.

17 — Randy Dobnak   RHP
Born: 01/17/95   Age: 25   Bats: R   Throws: R   Height: 6'1"   Weight: 230
Origin: Undrafted Free Agent, 2017

You know the story by now: Unfancied, undrafted, org guy strike-thrower makes good, makes the majors, starts in a playoff game. Dobnak didn't get his Hollywood ending against the Damn Yankees, but did put himself in position for a role on the 2020 Twins pitching staff. He's a real throwback, and it isn't just the *I Love the 90's* Rod Beck facial hair. In a high-spin, four-seam fastball up era, Dobnak pounds the bottom of the zone with a low-90s sinking fastball, and dares the launch angle superstars to try and lift it. It's an extreme groundball pitch with good sink and run. A mid-80s slider will show razor blade depth, but can get slurvy or back-up. There's a changeup as well, potentially average, and Dobnak will throw it to both righties and lefties. He's somewhat duplicative in profile with Devin Smeltzer, and they might be competing for the same spot in February. Dobnak doesn't have a pitch as good as Smeltzer's change. He doesn't have his left-handedness either, but he should get a shot at a heartwarming sequel this year.

18 — Matt Canterino   RHP
Born: 12/14/97   Age: 22   Bats: R   Throws: R   Height: 6'2"   Weight: 222
Origin: Round 2, 2019 Draft (#54 overall)

The Twins second round pick, Canterino is a big, physically maxed college arm with average fastball velocity that plays up due to his advanced command of the pitch and the plane on it he generates from his high-three-quarters slot. He pairs it with a slider in the mid-80s that features late cut. The command of the slider lags behind the fastball at present, but the offering is a potential plus pitch with refinement. Canterino will also use a humpy, 11-6 curveball on occasion. Canterino isn't the most athletic specimen and his delivery can be a bit hitchy as well. So while there's no reason to move him to the bullpen yet, I wouldn't be surprised if he ends up a solid 95-and-a-slider setup type.

19 Blayne Enlow   RHP
Born: 03/21/99   Age: 21   Bats: R   Throws: R   Height: 6'3"   Weight: 170
Origin: Round 3, 2017 Draft (#76 overall)

Enlow keeps on keeping on, not missing quite as many bats as you'd like with any of his five offerings. He can dial his fastball up into the mid-90s now, but fringy command makes it a bit too hittable. The cutter sits around 90, and flashes above-average, but can roll in a bit lazily too. He can be overly fond of trying to backdoor the low-80s slider, and the gloveside command isn't always there when he tries to back foot it to lefties. The curve and the change-up remain more show-me offerings, although the cutter is useful enough against as a crossover option. The frame's good. The delivery's fine. But we are going to have to wait a while longer for something to pop in the profile. The sum of the parts should get Enlow to a backend starter, but the math hasn't added up so far.

20 Edwar Colina   RHP
Born: 05/03/97   Age: 23   Bats: R   Throws: R   Height: 5'11"   Weight: 240
Origin: International Free Agent, 2015

Colina has mid-90s heat and can touch higher, but he prefers to throw his slider. Over and over and over again. He manipulates the pitch well, and it's a plus slider, but that's not an approach that is going to work long term as a starter. The fastball runs pretty true and batters seem pretty comfortable taking their hacks at it. The delivery has some effort, and the fastball command and control is below-average too. so let Colina loose in the pen where he can spam the breaker to either side of the plate, early in counts, behind in counts, to get ahead, for strikeouts, whatever.

Personal Cheeseball

Gabriel Maciel   OF
Born: 01/10/99   Age: 21   Bats: B   Throws: R   Height: 5'10"   Weight: 170
Origin: International Free Agent, 2016

Maciel came to the Twins in the same deal Jhoan Duran, and while he hasn't broken out to the same level, he's an intriguing outfield prospect. Generously listed at 5-foot-10, Maciel knows his game, he's a burner that is never going to hit for much power. He needs to hit the ball on the ground, or on a line, and run. Despite a wide open stance and leg kick, Maciel is short to the ball, and shows solid barrel control. There's enough bat speed to shoot fastballs over the second baseman's head, but the lack of physicality means he might not drive the ball enough to develop a true plus hit tool. He'll mitigate some of that by bunting his way on a dozen times a year or so. Like I said, he knows his game. His plus-plus speed makes him a solid enough center fielder, and while the lack of pop might limit him to more to a bench outfielder role, it feels like we are about due for another Ben Revere. Not a surprise he would come back as a Twin again.

Low Minors Sleeper

LMS

Luis Rijo RHP
Born: 09/06/98   Age: 21   Bats: R   Throws: R   Height: 6'1"   Weight: 200
Origin: International Free Agent, 2015

The third of the Yankees prospect Luises was dealt for Lance Lynn last summer. He's never had the premium raw stuff of Medina or Gil, but Rijo has the most advanced pitchability of the troika, and the stuff is solid enough. His fastball has ticked up into an average velocity band, but he's close to physically maxed, so it's unlikely there's too many more ticks to come. He throws effective strikes with it, and it's a lively pitch. Rijo works a full four-pitch mix with decent feel for everything, and his-mid 70s curveball has turned into more of an upper-70s power slurve with sharp two-plane action. That might give him the out pitch he's been missing and make a backend rotation role more likely. Keep your eye on this space for further developments.

Top Talents 25 and Under (as of 4/1/2020)

1. Royce Lewis
2. Jose Berrios
3. Brusdar Graterol
4. Alex Kirilloff
5. Byron Buxton
6. Fernando Romero
7. Miguel Sano
8. Jorge Polanco
9. Trevor Larnach
10. Nick Gordon

Max Kepler is the only member of last year's 25-and-under list to age out, but last year's no. 1 (Byron Buxton) and no. 3 (Miguel Sano) young talents had miserable 2018 seasons that saw them demoted to the minors. That makes ranking this year's 25-and-under options tricky, which is similar to trying to figure out where the Twins stand in general right now. They still have plenty of young major-league talent, with plenty of long-term upside, but the current crop has failed to establish itself as a winning core and it's hard not to turn your attention to the next wave.

Royce Lewis is a top 10 global prospect, the gem of a vastly improved farm system, and the base around which the next title-contending Twins team could be built. That those same things were said about Buxton, and to a lesser extent Sano, just a couple years ago is a reminder that not every prospect build is structurally sound. That both Buxton and Sano still qualify for this list, and might still be potential building blocks for the Twins when Lewis arrives this year or next, is also a reminder that a wave of talent can hit the same beach more than once.

Jose Berrios is the only member of the current young core to fully live up to the hype, or at least to do so without incident. Still only 24, he's coming off his first All-Star season and is the anchor of the staff. Fernando Romero lost his "prospect" status by five innings, but he won't be 24 until later this month and ended 2018 at Triple-A. Whether you consider him a prospect or a young major-leaguer, and whether you view him as a future starter or reliever, long term he's probably still closer to Brusdar Graterol as the Twins' best non-Berrios pitching hope than many think.

Buxton is impossible to rank definitively, especially compared to Alex Kirilloff, who's yet to reach Double-A. Last year, Kirilloff topping Buxton would've seemed absurd, yet it's reasonable now and if anything Kirilloff has the stronger case to be higher. Buxton is 25. He's an amazing center fielder and runner, but he's also a .230/.285/.387 hitter who generally looks lost at the plate. Similarly, how do you compare Miguel Sano, with his various flaws now exposed, to Trevor Larnach or even Brent Rooker, for whom a positive outcome might look like… Sano?

There's still a timeline where Buxton and Sano get back on track, rejoining Berrios as building blocks, and the Lewis-led next wave turns the Twins into contenders. It's not even that difficult to picture. Lewis, Sano, Jorge Polanco, Nick Gordon, and Rooker in the infield. Buxton flanked by Kirilloff, Kepler, and Larnach in the outfield. Berrios, Graterol, and Romero atop the rotation. But there's also a timeline where this wave dissipates further, leaving only one or two long-term pieces, and Twins fans pin their new hopes on Lewis/Graterol/Kirilloff instead of Buxton/Berrios/Sano.

Part 3: Featured Articles

The Baseball Is Juiced (Again)

Robert Arthur

This article originally appeared at Baseball Prospectus on April 5, 2019.

It started when the normally reliable Chris Sale got lit up for three homers by the Mariners in the Red Sox's season opener. It was part of a record number of taters that flew on Opening Day, as starters from Sale to Zack Greinke were taken deep by the handful. Then Christian Yelich hit a home run in each of his first four games, tying yet another MLB record, this one for consecutive games with a dinger to start a season.

It didn't take long for fans and players to begin whispering and tweeting about the baseballs being juiced again. It's early yet for us to come to any definitive conclusion about the 2019 season, but preliminary data shows that the baseball has returned to its aerodynamic peak. Whether that means this season will smash home run records like 2017 did remains to be seen.

Before home run explosion over the last few years, no one worried too much about the baseball's air resistance. While MLB and Rawlings (the company that manufactures the official baseballs) kept track of dozens of metrics to make sure that the ball was consistent from month to month, they didn't measure drag.

But drag is incredibly important in determining how likely a hitter is to knock one out of the park. As baseballs become more aerodynamic, they travel further given a certain initial velocity. A deep fly ball that might have been caught at the warning track can instead go into the first row of the stands. A three percent change in drag coefficient can work to add about five feet to a well-hit fly ball, which can in turn increase home runs league wide by an astounding 10-15 percent.

It's possible to measure the aerodynamics of the baseball using the pitch-tracking radars currently in place in each MLB ballpark. By calculating the loss of speed from when the pitch is released to when it crosses the plate, you can directly measure the drag coefficient on the baseball. I first wrote about the role of decreasing drag in boosting home runs in 2017, and MLB's commission of scientists and statisticians later confirmed that the more aerodynamic baseballs in use that year were largely to blame for the spike in home runs. The same commission rejected some alternate hypotheses, like rising temperatures and a league-wide boost in launch angle pushing more balls over the fence.

The current era has featured some large fluctuations in drag coefficient, leading to first an explosion in 2016 and 2017, and then a dialing back of homers last year. Curious about the record-breaking home run tallies in the last few days, I used the same methodology to measure the aerodynamics of the baseballs so far in 2019.

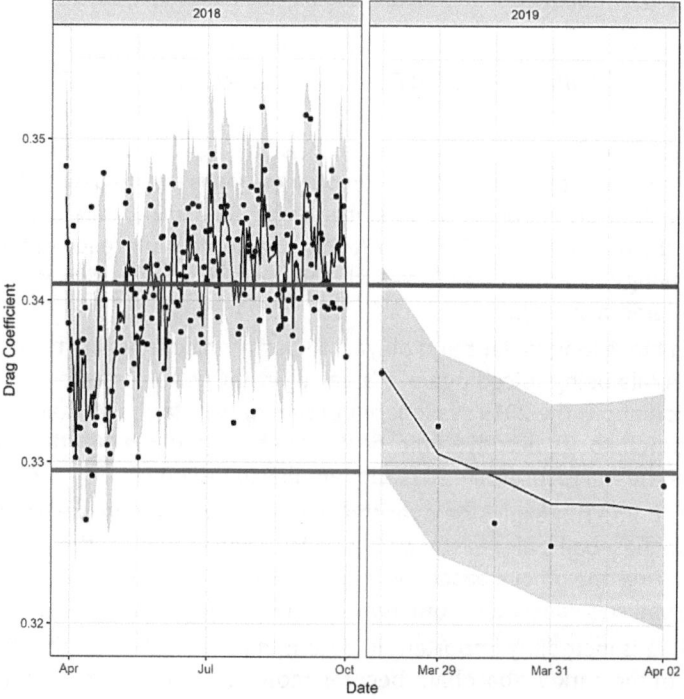

We're only a week into the 2019 season, but the drag numbers so far are among the lowest recorded in the last calendar year. With apologies for gory math, the current 2019 season average drag coefficient (the red line) would be below the 95 percent credible interval (the shaded area) for about nine-tenths of the 2018 season. (I used a Bayesian Random Walk model implemented in INLA to calculate these credible intervals, averaging the drag numbers in each game and adjusting for park.)

There were only a handful of six-day stretches in 2018 that had drag numbers below what we're seeing now, and most were in late June and early July. All of this means that 2019's data so far is quite a bit different than what we saw through most of last year.

These drag coefficients factor out the effects of temperature and air density, so they aren't a product of April cold. However, the numbers could be deceptive if the radars used to track pitches have changed from year to year. I consulted with some experts within baseball who were not aware of any specific modifications to the radar this year that could produce this pattern, but it's an important caveat of which to be aware.

On the one hand, it's only been six days, and we don't quite have the statistical basis to say that these drag coefficients are unprecedented compared to 2018. On the other hand, we've witnessed about 5,000 fastballs so far this season, so it's not as if our sample size is small. At least so far, the baseball has played like it's much more aerodynamic than it was last year. In fact, the current drag coefficient is really only comparable to 2017, when the baseballs were more aerodynamic than they had been in at least a decade.

It's not just fancy radar tracking indicating that the baseball is flying through the air more easily. The current number of home runs per game (as of this writing) is the highest it's been since the heady days of 2017, the year that teams and players broke dinger-related records everywhere you looked. That's especially remarkable considering that we're in what is typically the coldest part of the regular season, when lower temperatures and higher winds tend to suppress offense and keep balls in the air within the park. Comparing only from April to April, this year's rate of home runs per fly ball is even a little bit higher than it was in 2017.

With that said, the current measurements are no guarantee that 2019 will be another year of record-shattering homer hitting. The trouble with the drag measurements is that they are not consistent from June to August, from week to week, or even sometimes from day to day. Whether because of natural manufacturing variation or differences in the underlying supplies of cowhide and thread that go into the baseballs, drag has a tendency to fluctuate up and down over the course of a year. So the homers that fly in the first week of April wouldn't necessarily clear the fence a week later.

It's possible that this one-week drop in drag coefficient subsides and the baseball returns to its 2018 levels. On the other hand, it's almost equally probable that the ball becomes even more slippery and flies ever farther. Either way, it's clear that the baseball's air resistance is something to keep an eye on for the remainder of the 2019 season.

—*Robert Arthur is an author of Baseball Prospectus.*

The Moral Hazard of Playing It Safe

Craig Goldstein

This article originally appeared at Baseball Prospectus on August 6, 2019.

A couple days prior to the trade deadline, amidst a sea of tranquility posing as the lead up to the trade deadline, Bob Nightengale took to Twitter. Nightengale, who was probably wearing his pants backwards at the time, tweeted that MLB GMs were coming around on the idea that the unified trade deadline should be moved back from July 31 to August 15, so they could better assess their positions in the standings and whether they should buy or sell. To which I said:

This might strike some as reductive and churlish. And it might be that, but it isn't really wrong, either. Jeff Quinton wrote a great piece discussing the environmental factors that enable front offices to avoid risk without upsetting the apple cart within their own fanbases. I don't believe that it goes far enough, however. His article gives us the proper framework through which to understand why these behaviors have been allowed to seep into front offices throughout the league. Understanding the reasons behind these actions are different from excusing them, though, and GMs should not be let off the hook for their non-competitive approach to the trade deadline (much less the offseason).

⚾ ⚾ ⚾

It's fair to say that fans as a group have rarely, if ever, been pro-player. It is also fair to say that in the time during and following the Moneyball revolution, the pendulum swung from fans who cared intensely about winning in the moment (and thus might be intolerant of a rebuilding approach) to fans who supported building a team that could compete throughout multiple seasons, viewing the playoffs as a crapshoot, with the thought that getting multiple bites at the apple was a better approach than taking a bigger bite in any one season.

There's nothing wrong with that approach, and I still find merit in that argument. However, it seems that the pendulum has swung too far in that direction. Teams are overvaluing some of the individual factors that make themselves long-term contenders rather than attempting to seize a championship when given the opportunity. It's a difficult needle to thread.

And surely, they (and those in similar positions) would have liked another two weeks to clarify where they stand so as to better marshal their resources. We've all asked for a few more minutes when staring at a menu. But all of these GMs and front office personnel are where they are to make difficult decisions. They have proprietary data and internal analysts dedicated to understanding their position relative to the rest of the league, and how any move in the here and now impacts their long-term vision. To complain (if that report is accurate) that over half the season is not enough to properly assess their season is bullshit of the highest order. Move the deadline, and you'd simply have increasingly discounted trade offers because teams would be acquiring even less control of anyone they're acquiring, rental or not.

Major league front offices are behaving like the managers they lampooned two decades ago. They're effectively sacrificing a runner to second in the ninth inning—not because it's the correct move, but rather because it is safe. It used to be that the phrase "moral hazard" was used to describe general managers who made ill-fated, short-sighted decisions aimed at locking in wins and securing their jobs at the expense of their team's future. Now, general managers are guilty of committing moral hazards in the opposite direction, playing it utterly safe and terrified of becoming scapegoats.

In lieu of bold action, they opt to pussyfoot around a current window of contention, choosing instead to play the long game and stack up years of control like they're blocks in a game of Jenga. GMs pass on signing quality players in free agency because the back-end of the deal might look bad, and because they might be able to squeeze out 70 percent of the production from a player who costs a tenth as much. That's a safer investment, too, because it's also hard to prove a negative—it's impossible to prove that Manny Machado would make the Mets a playoff team in 2019-2020, but it's easy to say that the back half of Robinson Cano's contract sucks. Owners, who rule over GM's jobs, are also humans with human brain processes that will always make the so-called albatross contract uglier than the road not taken.

These days, GMs are remembered for the bad deals they make and the surplus value they generate, not the acquisition of expensive, necessary talents that meet their market worth (or fall slightly short while still providing significant on-field value). And front offices know that one or two expensive misfires can cost them their jobs, no matter how many good deals they make.

No front office exemplifies this ethos more than the Toronto Blue Jays. General Manager Ross Atkins had this to say following the Blue Jays underwhelming trade deadline:

This is by no means the first time that an executive will cite years of control to justify their actions, which is often just another way of saying "don't look at what we got, look at how much we got of it." Atkins touts quantity to elide the discussion of quality—either, that of the players acquired, or those given up. Remember: the other teams presumably value years of control, too.

Atkins also had some thoughts to offer regarding free agents back in early 2018:

This ignores, of course, whether the player can create enough value in the front end of a contract to justify the longer term of a deal, and the decline that often occurs in the back end. It also ignores whether the player can fill a need the team requires and put them in a position to compete for and win a championship. But as teams seemingly avoid contention at all, where they might end up having to consider and later justify some of these tough decisions, we still see risk-averse approaches.

Anthony Fenech's article on two trades that recently extended GM Al Avila didn't make got at this issue rather well:

> Passing on those deals was defensible: Both players had yet to break out and trading [Michael] Fulmer—a pitcher who appeared to be a future ace, no matter his injury concerns—would have taken serious gumption, opening Avila up to strong criticism.

Avoiding strong criticism is something each of us can understand as a motivation, but the avoidance of criticism only matters if that criticism is valid. In Fulmer's case, shoving his injury concerns aside affects not only the years that the team controls him (he is currently missing a full season due to Tommy John surgery) but also the quality of those seasons, as his knee and elbow injuries combined to dampen his effectiveness even when healthy enough to pitch. But it was easy to present the then-current image of Fulmer as a top of the rotation pitcher who the team had under its domain for the next five seasons as something to build around. The status quo isn't nearly as often second-guessed as a decision that disrupts it.

⚾   ⚾   ⚾

MLB GMs are risk-averse to a fault. They are ivy-educated and consulting firm-approved, and yet they can't seem to avoid leaving wins on the table in their all-consuming lust for a non-existent $/WAR championship. They are supposed to zig when everyone else zags, and not merely pay lip service to the idea of zigging through a calculated PR plan built on convincing the fan base their approach is novel when it actually apes most of their competitors. Instead they've become far more concerned with making safe, accepted-by-the-new-common-wisdom decisions, such that our prior understanding of what a moral hazard is has become inverted.

I can't blame them entirely, and not only because of the reasons that Quinton illuminated in his article, but also because of the damage wrought by the introduction of the second wild card (WC2) spot. MLB's desire to have more teams in playoff contention has sparked anti-competitive behavior. Teams know now that they do not need to swing big as they assemble their roster because there is a good chance that a mediocre team can either catch fire and capture a division, or muddle along until they back into the WC2.

Simultaneously, the one-game playoff has neutered the WC1, putting an entire season on the flip of a coin like some sort of baseball-obsessed Anton Chigurh. While the one-game playoff makes sense as a way to increase the value of winning a division, it also means that if a front office doesn't like its chances of overcoming a behemoth like the Dodgers or Astros in the offseason, they have few incentives to chase glory. Similarly, the relative inaction in the NL Central at the trade deadline—despite a wide open division—can be explained by the idea that any high-variance investment could still result in only a wild card (or worse) result, given the mere two months left in the season to make an impact.

⚾ ⚾ ⚾

As stated at the top, we should not confuse reasons for excuses. The implementation of the second wild card is just one of many environmental factors that influence how each front office operates. I am convinced that it is one of the larger factors, but I am also convinced that organizations need to shed the yoke of "efficiency at all costs" so that they can instead pursue competition, as the spirit of the game intends. Until they do, we're all deadline losers.

—*Craig Goldstein is an author of Baseball Prospectus.*

Index of Names

Adrianza, Ehire 18
Alcala, Jorge 99
Arraez, Luis 20
Astudillo, Willians 22
Avila, Alex 24
Baddoo, Akil 90
Bailey, Homer 46
Balazovic, Jordan 100, 113
Berríos, José 48
Blankenhorn, Travis 105
Buxton, Byron 26
Canterino, Matt 101, 118
Cavaco, Keoni 91, 113
Cave, Jake 28
Celestino, Gilberto 92, 115
Chacín, Jhoulys 50
Chalmers, Dakota 107
Clippard, Tyler 52
Colina, Edwar 119
Cruz, Nelson 30
Dobnak, Randy 54, 118
Donaldson, Josh 32
Duffey, Tyler 56
Duran, Jhoan 102, 112
Dyson, Sam 58
Enlow, Blayne 103, 119
Garver, Mitch 34
Gearrin, Cory 60
Gomez, Moises 93
Gonzalez, Marwin 36
Gordon, Nick 105, 116
Graterol, Brusdar 110
Gray, Seth 105
Hardy, Blaine 62
Hildenberger, Trevor 107
Hill, Rich 64
Holland, Will 105
Javier, Wander 94
Jax, Griffin 107
Jeffers, Ryan 105, 115
Kepler, Max 38
Kirilloff, Alex 95, 111
LaMarre, Ryan 105
Larnach, Trevor 96, 111
Lewis, Royce 97, 109
Littell, Zack 66
Maciel, Gabriel 105, 119
Maeda, Kenta 68
May, Trevor 70
Miranda, Jose 105
O'Rourke, Ryan 107
Ober, Bailey 104
Odorizzi, Jake 72
Pineda, Michael 74
Polanco, Jorge 40
Poppen, Sean 107
Raley, Luke 105
Rijo, Luis 120
Rogers, Taylor 76
Romero, Fernando 78
Romo, Sergio 80
Rooker, Brent 98, 117

Minnesota Twins 2020

Rosario, Eddie 42
Sands, Cole 117
Sanó, Miguel 44
Severino, Yunior 105
Smeltzer, Devin 82, 116
Stashak, Cody 84
Steer, Spencer 105
Thorpe, Lewis 86, 114
Urbina, Misael 118
Vallimont, Chris 107
Wade Jr, LaMonte 105
Wallner, Matt 105, 117
Wiel, Zander 105
Wisler, Matt 88